SKIING NEW MEXICO

Skiing New Mexico

A Guide to Snow Sports in the Land of Enchantment

DANIEL GIBSON
FOREWORD BY JEAN MAYER

University of New Mexico Press • Albuquerque

© 2017 by the University of New Mexico Press
All rights reserved. Published 2017
Printed in Korea
22 21 20 19 18 17   1 2 3 4 5 6

Library of Congress Cataloging-in-Publication Data

Names: Gibson, Daniel, author.
Title: Skiing New Mexico: A Guide to Snow
    Sports in the Land of Enchantment /
    Daniel Gibson; Foreword by Jean Mayer.
Description: Albuquerque : University of New
    Mexico Press, 2017. | Series: Southwest
    Adventure Series | Includes bibliographical
    references and index.
Identifiers: LCCN 2017005529 (print) | LCCN
    2017020907 (ebook) | ISBN 9780826357564
    (pbk. : alk. paper) | ISBN 9780826357571
    (E-book)
Subjects: LCSH: Skis and skiing—New
    Mexico—Guidebooks. | Ski resorts—
    New Mexico—Guidebooks. | New
    Mexico—Guidebooks.
Classification: LCC GV854.5.N43 G53 2017
    (ebook) | LCC GV854.5.N43 (print) | DDC
    796.9309789—dc23
LC record available at https://lccn.loc.
    gov/2017005529

Cover illustration: courtesy Angel Fire Resort
Series design by Lisa C. Tremaine
Composed in Minion Pro and Gotham

This book is dedicated to my mother, Virginia Whipple (and ski moms everywhere),
who got five kids clothed and equipped onto the ski slopes;
my father, David Gibson, who owned one of the early pairs of Head Standards
and helped grow the New Mexico ski scene;
and my wife, Kitty Leaken, who has accompanied me on many ski outings
and allowed me to explore my snow-filled passion oveer the years.

Contents

peterLamont.com

Foreword

I am often asked, "What is the magic of skiing in New Mexico?" There is no single answer to that question but rather a series of factors that produce such a great ski experience here.

First, it begins with the quality of the snow. As soon as I arrived here from Europe I discovered the wonderful snow—so light, so fluffy, so good! It is not always powder but still has a quality that is so much better than what I was used to. Because of the altitude and surrounding deserts, the snow doesn't have the moisture and the humidity of most snow. And, because of our southern latitude, the tree line is much, much higher than most ski regions, which protects our snow from wind and sun. In Europe you almost always ski above tree line. That can be tough.

Good year, bad year, there is always snow. Sometimes we have to wait for the big storms, but they always come. Never have we not had snow.

And yet we also often get to ski in sunshine. To ski in the sun most of the time is fantastic! Elsewhere you might ski in fog or clouds, in bitter cold. It taxes you.

Here we have a unique combination of abundant, or at least enough, snow and sunshine.

I also think that the lack of humidity means even our manmade snow is better than other regions'. This matters a lot. The snow we make creates a good base that lasts for the whole winter, with the natural snow on top.

Our geographic location also often provides us with early snow. Moisture moving off the Gulf of Mexico and Gulf of California meets cold fronts pushing down from Canada, and so we get solid snows in late fall, when other interior states are dry. How lucky we are!

The range and style of our ski areas is also broad, from Red River, where you gaze into Colorado, to Ski Apache, where you can see mountains in Mexico. The character of various areas is also diverse. For instance, novices are drawn to Angel Fire, but after a few days they venture over to Taos and find out there are so many possibilities there as well. People in Albuquerque may only have a few hours to ski, and they can be at Sandia Peak in a half hour. How easy that is! Some people prefer small areas, like Pajarito, or value low prices; others are looking for an international experience. The range of choices here is endless. Often I head over to Sipapu in the first weeks of the season because they do such a good job with snow-making. It's beautiful. I love it; it's full of young people and has a great feeling.

Another major factor in our appeal is the terrain, which is not artificial or controlled by humans like a carnival ride. The idea is not to make all the runs easy and readily accessible. We try to maintain a measure of challenge. Here, people come to experience the honest integrity of the mountain. We rough it up a bit, in part because our ski areas simply don't have the money to even out all the rough edges. The terrain here is more natural and organic, not manicured. We retain our hiking terrain, the super-steep and untracked slopes. Our terrain has an attitude, a mood that is very honest, and we sustain a love of the natural alpine world.

Here the simple lack of crowds is so refreshing. Elsewhere you might stand in lines and be pressed on all sides on the slopes. At Taos we are pushing to build skier numbers, trying to get back to the 5,000 skiers per day we experienced 30 years ago. We don't want to go beyond these numbers; we are not looking to turn this into a mass market. On our mountains, the skiers are spread out, which provides a quality experience.

Our New Mexico ski pioneers—people such as Ernie Blake, Pete Totemoff, Bob Nordhaus, Buzz Bainbridge, and so on—had this outlook, and their attitudes continue to shape our experience today. They were people drawn to adventure, a different calling, true mountain people. They were attracted not only to our snow, weather, and terrain but also to the sense of freedom here, the loose lifestyle and the refreshing mix of our various cultures—Hispanic, Native American, and European.

Our ski areas are also still mostly family owned, lacking a corporate mentality. People come here by choice because they do not want to go to a resort like Aspen or Deer Valley. Taos Ski Valley was created by skiers for skiers, not to bring the city to the mountains but, rather, to safeguard the integrity of the mountain and the skiing environment. This spirit is what makes us different and attractive to people.

Our professional ski community is very close, like a family. It's amazing to me that many of us have been working alongside one another for decades. I don't see the other areas as competitors; we are in this together. Our employees don't need to take a special class in how to be friendly—they just are. It comes from the heart. And most employees don't just drop in for one season. They grow up here, they live here; they don't come and go. I think that is very important.

Skiing here is a way of life, which has been created from the very beginning. The experience is not an ambience created by money or corporate directives. It is organic and heartfelt. From the very beginning, the people who created the ski areas here were driven by the skiing and a sharing of winter sports and the mountains, never as a means to get rich.

For me, that original spirit is maintained. So come enjoy the beauty, warmth, and charm of our mountain environment, where skiing is still what matters.

Jean Mayer
Taos Ski Valley
September 2016

Jean Mayer was born and raised in France, where he was the Junior National champion. Working after World War II at the German resort of Garmisch-Partenkirchen in Bavaria, where American GIs headed for holidays, he was befriended by many Americans who went on to hold prominent positions in the US ski industry, including Pete Seibert (founder of Vail) and members of New Mexico's fledgling ski community. This led to his being asked by Taos Ski Valley founder, Ernie Blake, to come to TSV as director of its famous ski school—considered one of the most progressive and effective in the nation—a position he has held for many years. In 1960 he and his family opened TSV's first hotel, the Hotel St. Bernard. For many years the St. B was the sole lodging in the valley and is still a central element of its character. Its copper-covered fireplace is the eternal flame of the valley, and Jean is the heart and soul of its unique ambience.

Acknowledgments

Thanks first to ski area managers Tom Long of Pajarito, Benny Abruzzo and Ben Abruzzo of Ski Santa Fe and Sandia Peak, Gordon Briner of Taos Ski Valley, Walt Foley and Linton Judycki of Red River, Gary Forrest of Sipapu, Mike Hess and John Kitts of Angel Fire, and Justin Roland of Ski Apache, who keep New Mexico skiing alive and like no other region in the nation. And a salute to Judy and John Miller, founders of Enchanted Forest Cross-Country Ski and Snowshoe Area.

Providing consistent edge pressure on the state's ski industry is George Brooks, executive director of the trade group Ski New Mexico. Brooks took the NCAA national championship as the University of New Mexico Lobo ski coach in 2004. Thanks for your support of my writing over the decades.

A big abrazo to Jean Mayer of Taos Ski Valley for his foreword to this book. I couldn't have hoped to get a better spokesperson for the sport in New Mexico, nor anyone more respected and loved.

I'd also like to thank writer Arin McKenna for input on the Pajarito chapter's dining options, Guy Jackson for his help with the Sandia material, Mary Ann DeBoer of the Chama Chile Ski Classic, and the professional assistance over the years of the Blake family of Taos—particularly Adriana, Alejandro, and Mickey.

For providing photos and help with research, I tip my hat to ski area staffers Deborah Owen at Sandia Peak and Ski Santa Fe, Candy DeJoia at Ski Santa Fe, Dave Smith at Taos Ski Valley, Stacey Glaser at Pajarito Mountain and Sipapu, Krysty Ronchetti at Angel Fire and her team at SJ Communications, Christy Germscheid at Angel Fire, Karen Kelly at Red River, and the Goins family at Enchanted Forest. Others who provided photos include Kitty Leaken, Megan Gallagher, and Rachel Swigart of Red River, Jared Bella at Taos Imagery, guide Marc Beverly, Mo Kaluta, Christiana Hudson, and Charlene Carp and the Bauserman Group of Reno, Nevada.

I'd also like to thank my editor at the University of New Mexico Press, John Byram, who promptly responded to all my long questions and helped guide this book to fruition, Kathleen Meyer for her careful copyediting, and UNM Press staffers Patricia Kanavy, Lisa Tremaine, Katherine White, and Jennifer de Garmo. Ashley Biggers, the writer and editor who developed the outdoor guidebook series this volume is a part of, thanks for lighting a fire under me to get this done! Also, gracias to ski writers Peter Kray and Eric Wagnon for their initial "thumbs-up" reviews of the manuscript.

Finally, I'd like to thank the various newspapers, and especially the *Santa Fe New Mexican*, for their ongoing publication of my weekly snow sports and travel column, Snow Trax, which led inexorably over the decades to this book. A special shout-out to the paper's magazine director, Deborah Villa.

Introduction

I grew up skiing in New Mexico, taking my first spills in the white realm just shy of my seventh birthday. This was the old Santa Fe Ski Basin, with lace-up leather boots and skis with wood edges for wee tykes. In the day lodge, today's Totemoff's bar, the smell of wet wool and the excited chatter of people coming and going filled the air.

I fell in love with it all then—the thrill when you stayed upright for a bit, rolling in the snow, scrambling up for another slide down; the fireplaces, the parents and kids; the tall, dark pines with their blankets of snow.

We skied a lot at the predecessor of today's Sandia Peak ski area, La Madera (The Woods), near Albuquerque. The area had one of the nation's longest T-bars, which constantly pitched kids, and adults, off into a thicket. We went to Taos every year after Christmas and stayed through New Year's, usually doubling up with other families into packed A-frame cabins and the valley's first condominiums. This is where I first met the Taos founders, people such as Ernie Blake and his wife, Rhoda; the Mayer brothers; Pete Totemoff; Walter Widmer; and many other founders of New Mexico's skiing culture.

Some winters I skied almost every weekend, often with our neighbors, who had 10 kids. My father helped finance the construction of the Sandia Peak Tramway, and so I was among those at its base the day it was dedicated in 1966. It is still an amazing feat of engineering and nerve. It also provides for arguably the nation's fastest city-to-slope skiing.

New Mexico is full of superlatives, from its history as a pioneer of skiing in the western United States to the possession of some of the world's lightest powder snow, born of our high-desert geography. In fact, Ski Santa Fe's base elevation, 10,350 feet, is the fifth highest in North America. Our altitude generally ensures skiing that is good to off-the-charts, often under a powerful, brilliant southwestern sun and bluebird skies.

There's great skiing from just south of the Colorado border in resorts like Red River, Angel Fire, and Taos in the mighty Sangre de Cristo Range. The southernmost leg of the range is home to tiny Sipapu and Ski Santa Fe, the latter just 15 miles from Santa Fe, "The City Different." West across the Rio Grande lies the Jemez Mountains, home to little-known Pajarito Mountain just outside Los Alamos, the Atomic City. Down south, near Ruidoso in the Sierra Blanca area of the Sacramento Mountains, not far from Billy the Kid's hangouts, is Ski Apache, just one of two ski areas in the nation owned by an Indian tribe. Almost-unlimited opportunities for cross-country and backcountry alpine touring exist here, often on terrain that's seen few or no other skiers.

But these stories and more will unfold in the chapters to come. I think you will find that skiing in New Mexico is something quite different from the industrial-scale resorts of Colorado and other known skiing centers. It still is something of the "Land of Mañana" (which here doesn't necessarily mean "tomorrow" but rather "not today"). So slow down, enjoy the 200-mile views from the summits of our peaks. Get into the quiet woods. Breathe in all that pine-factory oxygen. Enjoy a brew, a soak, a back rub, a plate of red-and-green enchiladas. Visit a museum or a thousand-year-old Pueblo village, or take a hike. Fall in the snow and roll around. It's all here, waiting for you.

If you are seeking yet more information about our ski scene, you might want to look for my weekly snow sports and travel column, Snow Trax, which has run in the *Santa Fe New Mexican* for more than 20 years. This book evolved out of that column, which covers the people, special events, news, and developments in the skiing realm of New Mexico and southern Colorado. Older columns can be found on my WordPress page (www.dbgibnumex.wordpress.com) and on my personal website (www.DanielBGibson.com). *¡Bienvenidos!* Welcome!

Author's Notes

I grew up on skis and have been writing about snow sports long before snowboarding came along, but I view them simply as different means of moving over snow. They provide slightly different sensations but I think of them as largely interchangeable. For simplicity's sake and to reduce redundancy, I have generally used the terms "skiing" and "skier," but their use should also imply "snowboarding" and "snowboarder."

Pricing details were current when this manuscript was submitted but are bound to change over time. I have used the term "at least" when describing prices to account for inflation, but the values give you a starting point for determining costs.

I plan to update this book over time, particularly its e-book version, so I'd love to hear from readers who spot errors or have suggestions for future editions or just want to say "hola." I can be reached at DanielGibsonNM@gmail.com.

Part One: Ski Area Profiles

Angel Fire Resort

Address: Physical: 10 Miller Lane, Angel Fire, NM 87710; Mail: PO Box 130, Angel Fire Resort, NM 87710

Ski Report: Online only

Information: 855-990-0194

Websites: Resort: www.angelfireresort.com; town of Angel Fire: www.angelfirechamber.org

Facebook: Angel Fire Resort

Twitter: @angelfireresort

Instagram: @angelfireresort

Operating Hours: 9 a.m.–4 p.m. Night skiing 4–8 p.m. peak nights

Season: Generally mid-December through late March

Mountain Profile

Base Elevation: 8,600 feet

Summit Elevation: hike-to 10,800 feet; lift-served 10,677 feet

Vertical Drop: 2,077 feet

Annual Snowfall: 210 inches

Area: 560 acres

Runs: 80 named

Longest Run: Headin' Home (2.5 miles)

Lifts: Seven (two high-speed quads, three double chairs, and two surface lifts)

Lift Capacity: 8,100 skiers per hour

Terrain Classification: Beginner: 21 percent; Intermediate: 56 percent; Expert: 23 percent

Terrain Parks: Three

Snowmaking: 52 percent of the runs

Seasonal Visits: 150,000 skiers per year

Backcountry Access Policy: Closed boundary

Season Highlights: One of the most original competitions on snow anywhere is the World Championship Shovel Races held here every February. Adults and kids ride standard aluminum shovels down a prescribed course, hitting speeds of 70 mph. Late January brings on the annual Big Ol' Texas Weekend, with steak-eating contests, live music, races, and other happenings. The resort also hosts several major competitive ski and snowboard events each winter, including the USASA Southwest Freeride Series and the TransAm Tour.

Webcams: At least three: at summit, at base, and in Liberation Park

Amazing Facts: Its name is said to be a translation of a phrase for the valley by the region's early residents, the Moache Utes, and from the reddish glow of morning and evening light on the mountains and valley air.

The Bottom Line: Angel Fire is home to the state's longest and fastest chairlift, the high-speed Chile Express; the state's only night skiing; the Polar Express tubing area; and an active terrain park program with cool comps, facilities, and personnel. It caters to families and beginning and intermediate skiers but has something for almost every taste.

Getting Here

DRIVING

The ski area is located in the Moreno Valley near Eagle Nest, on private land within the Carson National Forest. It is 94 miles north of Santa Fe, 154 miles north of Albuquerque, and 24 miles southeast of Taos.

If coming from Santa Fe, take US 285/84 north to Española, then NM 68 to Taos. On Taos's south edge take US 64 east over Palo Flechado Pass (elevation 9,101 feet) to NM 434. Turn right (south) and proceed a few miles to the Village of Angel Fire. The entrance to Angel Fire Resort is on the left and well marked.

If coming from the east (Texas or Oklahoma), from Springer on I-25, head north seven miles to NM 58, and turn west to Cimarron. Here turn left (west) onto US 64 and proceed through Eagle Nest to NM 234. Turn left (south)

and proceed a few miles to the Village of Angel Fire. The entrance to Angel Fire Resort is on the left and well marked.

If coming from Taos, from Paseo del Pueblo South, turn east onto US 64 over Palo Flechado Pass (elevation 9,101 feet) to NM 434. Turn right (south) and proceed a few miles to the Village of Angel Fire. The entrance to Angel Fire Resort is on the left and well marked.

Flying

The closest major airport is the Albuquerque Sunport, and commercial flights also land in Santa Fe, an hour closer. The private Angel Fire Airport, just three miles away, can accommodate almost any charter plane flying today. You can rent a car in Albuquerque (http:// www.abqsunport.com/getting-around/rental-cars/) or in Santa Fe (I suggest four-wheel drive if snowfall is predicted; https://santafe.org/Visiting_Santa_Fe/About_Santa_Fe/Getting_Around_Santa_Fe/) or take a paid shuttle (see below).

Train and Bus Links

Amtrak stops in Albuquerque, and near Santa Fe at Lamy.

There is also a commuter rail service, the **Rail Runner** (www.nmrailrunner.com), which operates multiple times a day from Albuquerque to downtown Santa Fe. It includes a bus link in Albuquerque to the airport. However, there is no bus service to Angel Fire.

Shuttles

Several companies run between Angel Fire and the Albuquerque airport. These include

Mountain View Shuttle: 575-770-8759, www.mountainviewshuttle.com (round trip at least $225)

Roadrunner Shuttle and Charter: 505-424-3367, www.roadrunnershuttleandcharter.com

Angel Fire Resort also provides a shuttle service from various parking lots and condominium complexes to the ski area base, 8:30 a.m.–5 p.m. daily. The condo stop fee is at least $1 per ride. It also runs a free shuttle between the Lodge at Angel Fire and the country club.

Maps

A good map of the village showing accommodations and other landmarks can be found at www.discoverangelfire.com/content/pdf/discover_map.pdf.

Services

Lift Tickets

Three "value periods" and three "peak periods" affect ticket prices down and up. Prices here are for "regular season" rates. Adult all-day lift tickets run at least $68, half day at least $54; teens (13–17), full day at least $58, half day at least $49; juniors (7–12), full day at least $48, half day at least $40. Free for children age 6 and younger, seniors over 70, and fifth graders skiing with a parent (fill out form online and bring a current report card). Night lift tickets are at least $24, or at least $12 with same-day ticket. Discounts are available for tickets purchased online at least three days in advance. The ticket office is located at the foot of the Chile Express chairlift. For details or purchasing tickets by phone, call 575-377-4320 or 855-990-0194.

For tickets pre-purchased either online or via phone (as well as preordered rentals or lessons), pick up your arrival packet at the reservations center directly in front of the rental shop.

Rentals

The resort-based rental shop, located below the Chile Express chair next to Slopeside Sports

and the Village Haus, opens at 8 a.m. Its regular rental skis or snowboards, plus boots and poles, cost at least $30 for adults and $20 for juniors (ages 7–12). The shop also carries a selection of premier skis (at least $40 for skis, boots, and poles). It also rents boards or skis on a half-day basis, or just skis, or just boots. Helmets run at least $10. Reservations can be made via phone (855-990-0194) or online.

Tuning

Complete tune-ups, edging, and waxing can be done in the rental shop at the base.

Retail Shops

Slopeside Sports in the base complex sells a wide range of apparel and accessories.

The Village of Angel Fire also has a handful of retail ski and snowboarding shops. Some of the options include

WinterSport Ski Shop (12 Aspen Street, 575-377-6612, www.wintersportsskishop.com), only a hundred yards from the base chairs, is the oldest and most experienced shop here. It offers demo packages for boarders and skiers, plus snow blades and helmets. Online reservations are encouraged. Open 8 a.m.–6 p.m. daily, with extended holiday hours. With a shuttle to the slopes, it can't be beat!

Cottam's (40 North Angel Fire Road, on the main access road, 575-377-3700, www.cottamsskishops.com) rents skis and boards (including high-performance models), boots, poles, snow blades, and apparel. They offer online registration, a reservation system, and tuning services. Opens at 7 a.m.

Village Ski Shop (26 Aspen, 575-377-2475 or 800-469-9327, www.villageskishop.com) has demo and regular packages, and offers free rentals to those taking a lesson for the first time at Angel Fire. They also rent cross-country skis and snowshoes. No apparel rentals. Free parking. Opens at 8 a.m., with extended peak period hours, and discounted online reservations.

Trailhead Ski and Bike Shop (3420 Mountain View Boulevard, 575-337-1010, www.aftrailhead.com) offers rentals, tuning services, advance registration, and sale of hardware and soft goods. You can pick up gear at 3 p.m. the day prior.

Snowblaze Ski Shop (14 Five Spring Road, 575-377-2377 or 866-313-2377, www.snowblazeskishop.com) offers a convenient location just across the street from the base chairs. Established in 1990, it offers free on-slope overnight storage, (limited) free parking, and good rates.

Other village options include **Winter Sports Ski Shop**, **High Country Ski Rental**, and **Ski Tech Rentals**.

Ski School

Angel Fire has a notable ski school, with the smallest class sizes in the region, the longest on-snow time, and the fastest registration process. Classes sell out and are capped at a certain number. Kids are issued GPS locators.

For first-timers skiers or snowboarders age 13 and up, lift ticket and a two-hour group lesson in the morning and another in the afternoon costs at least $109 (regular season) or $119 (peak periods). Add at least $10 for rentals.

For skiers or boarders 13 and older who've mastered the basics of turning and stopping, an advanced or expert two-hour class and all-lift ticket will cost at least $119 (regular season) or $129 (peak periods). Add at least $10 for rentals. For those age 13 and up, buying their own ticket and with their own equipment, a half-day lesson costs at least $59, or a full day at least $89.

The Little Chiles program is designed for kids ages 4–6 and includes more time spent on the snow, all rental gear (including helmets),

instruction, and lunch. It costs at least $149 (regular season) and $159 (peak periods). Reservations required: 855-990-0194.

For skiers ages 6–9, the daylong Mountain Explorers program of group instruction, lunch, rentals, and ticket costs at least $149 (regular season) or $159 (peak periods). A similar program, Mountain Adventures, for skiers ages 10–12, offers the same elements at the same cost. Young snowboarders, ages 6–12, can take a similar program at the same cost.

Private lessons are also available to any skier ages 3 and up, or snowboarder ages 5 and up. Lessons can run from one to three hours. As many as four people can be included. A one-hour private ski or snowboard lesson costs at least $109 (regular season) or $119 (peak periods); two hours at least $199 (regular season) or $209 (peak periods).

The area also offers daily early-bird (prior to 9 a.m.) and sunset lessons (after 4 p.m., when night skiing is on); an hour costs at least $109 (regular season) or $119 (peak periods).

Reservations are recommended for all lessons during peak periods and must be made at least 48 hours in advance. Call 855-990-0194 for details.

Adaptive Ski Program

Angel Fire offers private lessons and equipment rentals to serve a broad range of disabled skiers and snowboarders. Reservations at least three days prior are recommended.

Childcare

Snow Bear Camp, the resort's childcare program, runs 8 a.m.–4 p.m. daily for kids ages 6 weeks–11 years. The program includes a nutritious lunch, snacks, and—for those capable—at least one hour spent skiing in a separate safe zone for kids with a magic carpet lift. The center is located just above the Chile Express chair. A full day costs at least $169 (regular season) or $179 (peak periods). For details, call 575-377-4320 or 855-990-0194.

Mountain Tours

Free one-and-a-half-hour tours of the mountain are offered on weekends from January to close of the season. The basic layout of the ski area is given, plus tips on local history, flora, and fauna. Meet guides dressed in bright-yellow jackets at the top of the Chile Express chair. Must be intermediate level to join.

Lockers

Coin-operated lockers are found on the second level of the base complex. Baskets are also available in the rental shop.

Cell Phone Service

Excellent

First Aid

There is a ski patrol center located at the top of the Chile Express chair, another at the base of the Southwest Flyer chair. Call 575-377-4209 for help on the mountain. There's also an **UltiMed Center** (575-377-1805) in the base complex that serves all urgent care needs.

ATMs

Located in the grocery store in town

Background

Taos Ski Valley gets most of the print media attention in northern New Mexico, but its neighbor to the southeast, Angel Fire Resort, is the real Cinderella, especially in an exceptional snow year. You won't find huge egos hucking cliffs here; most folks are from Amarillo or other Texas locales, along with Albuquerque residents with a cabin or second home. The majority of skiers and boarders here stick to the groomers and extensive intermediate and beginner runs. But this means those who love untracked powder will find runs all to themselves and days of silent cruising through solo glades and down steep pitches.

The roots of Angel Fire Resort began growing in 1954 when Roy and G. F. LeBus of Wichita Falls, Texas, bought the 10,000-acre Monte Verde Ranch in the beautiful Moreno Valley on north-central New Mexico. This was followed a few years later by acquisition of the 15,000-acre Cieneguilla Ranch, once part of the vast Maxwell Land Grant. Following a visit to Vail, Colorado, the family was inspired to create a ski area. Runs were cut, lifts were installed, and all was, apparently, ready for business in December 1966. But unexpected problems arose with the lifts, so some 600 paying holiday guests were bused to the back side, where a Thiokol Spryte snowcat carried them uphill. Everyone had a great time munching on hot dogs and burgers cooked over a huge bonfire. Later that season, the back-side lifts began turning. However, the next year financial problems entirely stymied operations. The resort really got off the ground for the 1968–1969 season and has functioned ever since. The LeBus family sold its investment in 1972.

Angel Fire—like Red River just to the north and Ski Apache down south—is very popular with Texas and Oklahoma skiers due to its relative proximity to them. A drive market, it focuses on providing good value and activities for families. In fact, in 2015 it was selected as one of the 25 best ski resorts in America for families by *Vacations Guides of America*. Thus, it offers a large range of accommodations, with cooking facilities and a limited restaurant scene. Many accommodations are close enough to the slopes to allow walking in and out, which is a nice feature—park the car and forget about it!

The resort is mostly intended for beginner and intermediate skiers, but it does have a few really tough, shortish runs, a handful of hike-to slopes offering deep powder, and a few glades for advanced skiers. Its terrain parks are arguably the best in New Mexico, and it has the only night skiing operation in the state. It is also home to some unique annual events.

The views from the summit are truly a sight

to see, with the Moreno Valley spread out below you and the Sangre de Cristo Range to the west, including the state's highest point, Wheeler Peak (13,159 feet).

The Village of Angel Fire grew up alongside the resort. It was incorporated in 1986 and has about 1,200 year-round residents.

Mountain Highlights

Beginner Runs

First-timers should learn the basics at the bottom of the mountain on the runs **High Road** and **Dream Catcher**, which are served by their own short and easygoing lifts.

Once stopping and turning are mastered, skiers can catch the speedy Chile Express to the summit. Here they have the option of returning to the base on the very simple run **Headin' Home** or skiing off into the "back side" on **Highway**. Linked to **Hallelujah** or **La Bajada**, this provides access to the Southwest Flyer chair and a return to the summit.

Intermediate Runs

With more than half its terrain classified as intermediate, Angel Fire is a great place for such skiers or boarders. Most of the front side consists of intermediate runs, and about half the back. On the front, **Bodacious** is a fun series of short drops that bring you back to the base. Another is **Prospector** to **Jasper's**, ending under the Chile Express chair line.

On the back side, check out **Hully Gully**, **El Sol**, and **Fat City**, all paralleling the Southwest Flyer chair. Farther along the cat track Highway are **Arriba** and **Baa-da-Boom**.

Expert Runs

One of my favorite runs here is **Nice Day**, on the back side. Even strong intermediate skiers might enjoy its long, even descent with great views to the north. Some of the steepest, though short, pitches—**Minder Binder**, **Charisma**, and **Hari Kari**—are found just to its side.

Also on the back side are three hike-to runs, **Baa-da-Bing**, **Detonator**, and **Nitro**. They require a walk from the Southwest Flyer, gaining 150 vertical feet over a distance of three-quarters of a mile. Of the three, Nitro is the steepest and longest option; all are worth the 15-minute or so hike to reach them.

But the coolest expert runs of all might be

the seldom-skied **Maxwell's Grant** and **Silver Chute** off the Chile Express. They require lots of snow to open, but when they're on they are special: steep, narrow, and overlooked by most skiers here. The downside is you have to ski all the way to the bottom and come back to the summit to get another shot at them. Also at the very top under the Chile Express is **Domingo**, which has a great pitch and an eaglelike view over the valley. But it gets wind scoured and baked by afternoon sun so is rarely open. If it's skiable, get it while you can!

Powder

I had one of all-time best in-bounds powder days here during a huge storm cycle in 2015 when five feet fell in five days. And since most skiers here avoid powder, you can have run after run to yourself. At one point I stopped on **Nitro** on the back side, thrust my pole into the snowpack up to my elbow, and did not hit bottom. On days like those, you can ski anywhere and enjoy the powder, but also notable are **Maxwell's Grant** and **Silver Chute**, **Nice Day**, and **Angel's Plunge**.

Bumps

Almost all of Angel Fire's intermediate runs are regularly groomed and lack moguls, so to find bumps you'll need to visit some of the expert runs. On the front side this might include **Sluice Box** and **Glory Hole**. On the back side, hit **Nice Day** and other expert runs. Check the grooming reports to determine what expert runs have not been groomed, and head there.

Trees

The resort is continually adding gladed terrain; it's up to 30 acres or so now. On the back side are **Shane's**, **Bear**, and **Eagle** glades, all classified as advanced. On the front side, between Thumb and Prospector, is **Elk Glade**, which is suitable to cautious intermediate skiers.

Cruisers

Much of Angel Fire is cruising terrain, such as the front side's long return to base run **Headin' Home**. A nice alternative is **Bodacious**, or **Bodacious** to **Gusto Grande**, or **Lower Free Flight** to **Lower Jasper's** with its fun rollers. On the back side, seek out **Highway** to **Baa-da-Boom** to **Short Fuse**, or the well-traveled **Hully Gully**. Check the daily grooming report for details on what's been freshly worked, and head to those runs.

Terrain Parks

Angel Fire has arguably the most ambitious and extensive park program in the state. **Night Rider Park** is on **Exhibition** at the bottom of the mountain, and so it is accessible to riders during night-skiing evenings (see below). **Sweet Street** is the beginners' park and is found along the bottom of **Headin' Home**. The advanced complex, **Liberation Park**, is located atop the mountain and includes progressive lines with jumps, rails, and boxes, plus its own short lift, Chair 3. It attracts serious athletes from around the region and hosts some significant annual competitions.

Night Skiing

This is the only area in the state to offer night skiing, which spans about 50 acres and includes a terrain park. It operates on Friday and Saturday nights 4 p.m.–8 p.m., as well as all holiday and peak period nights. It costs at least $24, or at least $12 if you have a same-day lift ticket.

Dining

On the Mountain

On the mountain are three options. The **Summit Smokehouse** (575-377-4371) sits at the top of the Chile Express and Chair 3. With indoor and outdoor seating, it has beautiful views off its wraparound deck. It specializes in barbecue but serves other foods and snacks, plus beer, wine, and mixed drinks. At the bottom of the Southwest Flyer is the **Dog House** (575-377-4283), open weekends and during peak periods. It serves snacks and, weather permitting, outdoor-grilled brats, dogs, and burgers, plus beer and wine. And at the base of the Chile Express chair is the **Buzz**, serving hot and cold beverages, and snacks.

Below the Chile Express, on the lower level of the base complex, is the **Village Haus** (575-377-4242), open for both breakfast and lunch with simple cafeteria-style dining—like burgers, dogs, pizza, soups, salads, and sandwiches, plus a full bar.

While not right on-slope, there are a handful of other places to eat in the immediate base area. The **Sunset Grill** (10 Five Springs Road, just a few steps uphill from the ski area drop point or the base chair, 575-377-6681), is a great find. With a deep legacy, it has an alpine look and feel, such as a nice stone fireplace. It serves lunch and dinner and has a full bar. Lunch can range from tortilla soup or green chile pork stew to a salad, sandwich, or handmade burger; dinner options include pesto pasta, blackened chicken, and rancher's pie. Appetizers include edamame, hummus, and green chile cheese fries.

The Lodge at Angel Fire provides several choices. **Legends Grill** (level 2, 575-377-4201) dishes up burgers, pizza, and comfort foods like chicken-fried steak, plus a wide variety of

beers, wine, and cocktails. It's open for dinner daily. **Chianti's** (level 2, 575-377-4201) serves pizza and salads for dinner on weekends and peak periods. The **Lift** (lobby level, 575-377-4234) serves Starbuck's coffee, tasty breakfast burritos, delicious quiche, and fresh pastries for breakfast, and a slate of sandwiches, wraps and melts, and soups at lunch. Beer and wine are also available. It is open 7 a.m.–4 p.m., and extended hours during holidays.

In Town

There are some other places to dine away from the immediate base area; a few are in easy walking distance for dinner, but most require a vehicle.

Pub 'n Grub (52 North Angel Fire Road—the main access route—575-377-2335), despite its simple name, is surprisingly refined and delicious. Chicken pot pie, exceptional fish and chips, wedge salads, nightly specials, steaks, some New Mexican dishes like green chile stew, and desserts like crème brûlée. Home of the Scotch egg (green chile sausage wrapped around a hard-boiled egg, breaded, deep-fried, and served with homemade mustard). Fast and friendly service, plus a full bar and some TVs for sports broadcasts—what more do you need? The Larson family endeavor is open just for dinner, 5 p.m.–9 p.m.

Elements (100 Country Club Drive, 575-377-3055, www.angelfireresort.com/dining) in the very attractive country club with its impressive copper roof, is another excellent choice. It houses both a fine restaurant, with an 1,800-bottle wine cellar and an airy, contemporary bar with its own menu. The restaurant menu, under the supervision of Chef Kevin McCaffrey, is also available in the bar. Dinner entrees include rack of lamb, maple leaf duck, seared salmon, pork tenderloin, fine steaks and roast beef, plus novel side dishes and sauces. The bar menu runs from pot stickers and wings to pulled pork sandwiches, handmade burgers, pasta of the day, and fish and chips. The restaurant and bar are closed on Mondays. The resort runs a free shuttle to the club.

H2 Uptown (48 North Angel Fire Road, 575-377-1200, www.opentable.com/h2-uptown) serves a variety of steaks, novel fare like trout

such as the delicious meat loaf or gumbo plus hearty sides like whole baked potatoes, green chile potato cheese soup, and homemade desserts. Also known for good, friendly service, and they do takeout and delivery. Open for lunch and dinner. Closed Sundays and Mondays.

Lodging

With its high concentration of families, Angel Fire is loaded with condominiums and house rentals.

The **Lodge at Angel Fire** (10 Miller Lane, 855-990-0194, www.angelfireresort.com/lodging/lodge) is the resort's "signature" accommodation. Located just below the base facilities, it offers super simple walk-to access up a few sets of stairs. Its attractions include a small pool and hot tub (super popular at the end of the day), a fitness center, free Wi-Fi, several dining options (see Dining) and bars (see Nightlife). Rooms vary from standard setups to suites with immense bathtubs. The lodge also rents out homes and one- to three-bedroom condos, some right next to the property and others farther away. These are fully furnished, with equipped kitchens, fireplaces, bed linens, and other amenities. The lodge offers discounts for groups of 20 or more.

The resort also operates the **Angel Fire RV Resort** (27500 US 64, 575-377-4471, 855-421-0308, www.angelfireresort.com/lodging) year-round. Ranked among the best in America by Good Sam, it includes a hot tub, free Wi-Fi, 40-channel DIRECTV, guest laundry, fire pits, horseshoe pits, and 102 paved spaces for all kinds of RVs.

Discover Angel Fire (800-566-8247, www.discoverangelfire.com) is a central source of reservations, including hotels, motels, condos, houses, and cabins.

There are also many listings on **Airbnb** and **VRBO**, and yet another option is making a call to Brenda Johnson of Brenda's Property Management (575-377-5917, www.angelfire-lodging.com). Cheaper accommodations can be found in Eagle Nest, just ten minutes from Angel Fire.

scampi, and local dishes such as blue corn enchiladas and posole, plus unusual appetizers like elk sliders, bacon-wrapped shrimp, and crab mac and cheese. The restaurant is hidden on the back side of the building it occupies, so don't be put off by the faceless exterior. Happy hour runs 4 p.m.–6 p.m.

The **Bakery Café** (3420 Mountain View Boulevard / NM 234, 575-377-3992) is a terrific spot for a quick breakfast and good coffee or tea. Omelets, burritos, pastries (including apple fritters), juices, and other morning fare are served all day. Lunch includes a hearty BLT and New Mexican dishes. Reasonably priced and its nice staff start the day out right.

The **Pizza Stop** (1 North Angel Fire Road, 575-377-6340), just a few minutes' walk from the Lodge at Angel Fire, specializes in pies and does a great job with them. Open for lunch and dinner daily. Serves beer and wine and has a speedy takeout service.

Hail's Holy Smoked BBQ (3400 Mountain View Boulevard / NM 234, 575-377-9938) does barbecue right (ribs, brisket, sausage, turkey, all smoked on site), along with daily specials

Nightlife

With its family focus, there's not much nightly entertainment here. Après-ski, the **Village Haus** in the base complex fills up, with people often grooving to a live band during peak periods.

The **Lodge at Angel Fire** also has two bars, **Legends Grill** and the **Lift**; the former presents live music every weekend night.

Zebadiah's (on NM 434, about 1.5 miles from the ski area, 575-377-6358) is the oldest bar/restaurant in the area, rocking along since 1986 or so. For many years it was the only place open year-round. With walls festooned with farming implements, ranching memorabilia, and antique toys, it's a down-home place. It provides live music on Fridays, plus pool and darts and large-screen TVs for catching a game. But food here is slow to come out, and not why you should visit.

The owners of the **Pub 'n Grub** also opened a microbrewery in 2016, **Enchanted Circle Brewing Company** (20 Sage Lane). It is open Thursdays through Sundays, and daily in peak periods, 4 p.m.–9 p.m., and serves light food.

Other nightlife possibilities can be found in the towns of Taos and Red River, each about 45 minutes away.

In Addition to Downhill Skiing

Cross-Country Skiing

The excellent **Angel Fire Nordic Center** operates out of the **Angel Fire Country Club** (100 Country Club Drive, 575-377-4488, www.angelfireresort.com/activities) under the able direction of Joe Distefano. You can rent all needed gear here, including snowshoes, take a group or private lesson, and cruise out on a 15-kilometer network of trails groomed for both classic-style and skate-style skiers. The trails gently descend a hill and wind out in long easy loops onto the valley floor, then circle back, encompassing some ten acres altogether. Various legs can be linked up to keep you out for hours. It is open weekends (depending on conditions) 10 a.m.–4 p.m., with extended hours during peak periods.

The country club is also the site of a low-angle area for **sledding**, and a separated snow-play area, perfect for children ages 5–12. Angel Fire Resort runs a free shuttle between the lodge and the country club, providing convenient access. The country club has a restaurant and bar (see Dining), so you can spend an afternoon, morning, or all day enjoying a visit here.

A day pass costs at least $18 for adults and $10 for kids (ages 12 and under). Rental gear costs the same, as do snowshoes. A one-hour lesson costs at least $20 for adults and $10 for kids. A sledding pass costs at least $5.

Tubing

In addition to the low-key sledding at the country club (see above), the resort operates the state's most ambitious tubing program, the **Polar Coaster**, at the base of the ski area. It operates daily 12 p.m.–6 p.m., with extended peak period hours. It features six individual lanes running 900 feet in length, and a surface lift to carry you up. The cost is at least $20 an hour. Kids must be at least 42 inches tall to participate. Call 844-218-4107 to make reservations.

Snowshoeing

Miles of picturesque, isolated trails lace the Moreno Valley near Angel Fire. Some climb into foothills of flanking mountains, providing awesome views north up the valley to Baldy Peak (12,441 feet), and across the valley to Wheeler Peak. You can rent snowshoes at both the **Angel Fire Nordic Center** (see Cross-Country Skiing section above) or the **Village Ski Shop**. A local organization, **Moreno Valley Trekkers** (www.home.earth-link.net/~mvtrekkers), leads weekly guided outings open to visitors.

The country club (see Cross-Country Skiing section above) also rents snowshoes and has miles of easygoing, well-marked trails with stellar views just outside its doors.

Snowmobiling

There are several companies that provide snowmobiling trips in the area, including **Angel Fire Excursions** (3629 NM 434, next to George's Barber Shop, 575-377-2799). They offer trips of two to three hours, plus rental clothing and boots. One-day advance registration is suggested. Must be a minimum age of 16 with a valid license to operate.

Ice Fishing

Eagle Nest Lake, less than 30 minutes away, is New Mexico's premier ice fishing site. It harbors rainbow trout, pike, kokanee salmon, and perch. The **Eagle Nest Marina** (575-377-6941) can rent special fishing rods and power augers for drilling your fishing hole and can sell you a license. To check on ice conditions, call the marina or **Eagle Nest State Park** (575-377-1594).

Horse-Drawn Sleigh Rides

Offered by Nancy Burch's **Roadrunner Tours** (575-377-6416, www.rtours.com), these horse-drawn sleigh rides can range from several hours to chuck wagon lunch outings.

Pajarito Mountain

Address: Physical: 370 Camp May Road, Los Alamos, NM 87544; Mail: 397 Camp May Road, Los Alamos, NM 87544

Ski Report: 505-662-5725

Information: 505-662-5725, www.ski@skipajarito.com

Website: www.skipajarito.com

Facebook: Pajarito.Mountain

Twitter: @skipajarito

Instagram: @skipajarito

Operating Hours: Open Wednesdays through Sundays and federal holidays, 8 a.m.–4 p.m., with lifts beginning at 9 a.m.

Season: Generally Thanksgiving through Easter (with occasional later openings)

Mountain Profile

Base Elevation: 9,000 feet, lodge at 9,200 feet

Summit Elevation: hike-to 10,440 feet

Vertical Drop: 1,440 feet

Annual Snowfall: 137 inches

Area: 750 acres (about 325 skiable)

Runs: 40 named

Longest Run: Evershine (one mile)

Lifts: Six (one quad, one triple, three doubles, one surface)

Lift Capacity: 6,500 skiers per hour

Terrain Classification: Beginner: 20 percent; Intermediate: 50 percent; Expert: 30 percent

Terrain Parks: Two

Snowmaking: About 20 percent of the runs, including beginner and high-traffic zones (about 35 acres)

Seasonal Visits: Number not available

Backcountry Access Policy: Closed boundary; skiing outside boundary prohibited unless registered with ski patrol

Season Highlights: In early February, Pajarito usually presents its K2 Women's Weekend, with speakers, demos, clinics, free lessons to never-evers, a silent auction, and a dinner dance party, all to benefit New Mexico cancer programs. Later in February it hosts Telebration, a day dedicated to telemark skiers, with gear demos and clinics by PSIA level 3 instructors. It also holds a couple of brew fests every winter that focus on local and regional beer masters.

Webcams: One, with seven near and distant viewpoints

Amazing Facts: The international group of men and women who built the world's first nuclear weapons helped launch and popularize skiing here in the 1940s.

The Bottom Line: Pajarito (Little Bird) Mountain is a fun, smallish, very affordable ski area. It is rarely crowded but provides excellent powder skiing during a substantial winter and some of the state's most renowned bump runs. Set in the lovely Jemez Mountains near Los Alamos, dubbed Atomic City, Santa Fe is just an hour away.

Getting Here

Driving

The ski area is located in the Jemez Mountains five miles west and above Los Alamos, about one hour from Santa Fe.

To get there from Santa Fe, head north out of town on US 84/285 for 16 miles to Pojoaque, and turn left (west) onto NM 502. Proceed in Los Alamos to the Y, a split intersection on the east edge of downtown, and bear left onto Trinity Drive through downtown to Diamond Drive (NM 501). Turn left, cross Omega Bridge, and turn left again. Proceed through the Los Alamos National Laboratory security checkpoint (open to the public, but picture ID is required), and continue straight ahead on NM 501 a few minutes past another checkpoint, and turn right onto West Road, then quickly left onto Camp May Road. Proceed three miles to the ski area. The old Camp May Road has some steeper than regulation pitches, and some exposed points, so four-wheel drive on a snow day is strongly recommended.

Flying

The closest major airport is the Albuquerque Sunport, and commercial flights also land in Santa Fe daily. The drive from Albuquerque to Santa Fe town is one hour. You can rent a car in either Albuquerque (http://www.abq sunport.com/getting-around/rental-cars/) or Santa Fe (https://santafe.org/Visiting_Santa_ Fe/About_Santa_Fe/Getting_Around_ Santa_Fe/).

Train and Bus Links

Amtrak stops at Lamy, 20 minutes south of Santa Fe.

There is also a commuter rail service, the **Rail Runner** (www.nmrailrunner.com), which operates multiple times a day from Albuquerque to downtown Santa Fe. It includes a bus link in Albuquerque to the airport.

A public bus service operates between Santa Fe and Los Alamos. For details, see www.RideTheBlueBus.com. However, you will still need a lift from Los Alamos to the ski area itself, and there is no bus service.

Services

Lift Tickets

Adult all-day all lifts tickets run at least $49, teens (ages 13–20) at least $42, kids (ages 7–12) at least $34, seniors (ages 60–69) at least $42. Beginner tickets run at least $24. Half-day adult tickets are at least $39 and run 9 a.m.–12:30 p.m. and 12:30 p.m.–4 p.m. Skiers older than 69 or younger than 7 ski for free. It holds occasional weekday ticket discounts, including Carload Days (at least $99 for up to six skiers) and Thursday Local Appreciation Days (no ID is required, but you must ask for the deal). Active duty military ski for half price. There are no discounts for multiple day tickets. Group rate discounts for parties of ten or more are available.

Rentals

Pajarito's rental skis, boots, and poles run at least $22 for adults (ages 13 and up) and $17 for youth; snowboards run at least $25 for adults and $20 for youth. It also rents snow blades, and just skis, snowboard, or boots. Helmets run at least $20. The rental shop is in the lower level of the main lodge.

There are two options for rentals in Santa Fe.

Alpine Sports (121 Sandoval Street, 505-983-5155, www.alpinesport-santafe.com), Santa Fe's oldest ski shop, launched in 1963 and provides excellent customer service, a wide range of rentals (including high-end demos), sales of clothing and accessories, and excellent tuning work.

Ski Tech (905 South St. Francis Drive, 505-983-5512, www.skitechsantafe.com) rents skis, boards, and boots and poles, as well as snowshoes, snow pants, bibs, and helmets. It offers the city's only rental delivery service. Economy ski packages begin at $29 a day; premium demos at least $45. They also do tune-ups.

Tuning

A complete tune-up at the ski area runs at least $40, a waxing at least $10. Located in the rental shop in the main lodge.

Retail Shops

Small shop in the Lodge building with essential skiing basics

Ski School

Pajarito offers ski and snowboard lessons. A group class for first-timers, including equipment rentals, runs at least $50 for two hours, or $68 for four hours. Beginner packages run a bit more. Private lessons cost at least $65 per hour, or at least $200 for a full day.

Adaptive Ski Program

None

Childcare

None; children's ski school available

Mountain Tours

None

Lockers

Day lockers found in the rental shop

Cell Phone Service

Excellent

First Aid

Located to the west of the base lodge, facing the access road; 505-662-1991

Background

People have been skiing on the slopes above today's town of Los Alamos for many decades. In the 1930s, before there was a town, students and faculty from the Los Alamos Ranch School would spend a week every spring at Camp May, climbing and skiing. The first lift, at a spot called Sawyer's Hill, came in 1944 after the founding of Los Alamos as the center for the development of the atomic bomb and the infusion of many European scientists and their skiing culture. This included some backcountry forays. A historic photo shows physicist Enrico Fermi standing on the shoulder of Pajarito Peak with Valles Grande in the background. The ski operation, with a few rope tows, was moved to its present location in the winter of 1957–1958 through the superhuman effort of an all-volunteer crew. Runs were cut, trees bucked and slash burned, lifts raised. In 1962 a 3,500-foot T-bar climbing 1,105 vertical feet was erected, followed by pomas and in 1976 by the first chairlift. Volunteers continue even today on thinning projects in the woods between runs.

But Pajarito was largely unknown even to most New Mexicans for many years due to the general secrecy surrounding the Atomic City. And then it was plagued by many years of no to low snowfall, culminating in the Los Conchas fire of 2011, which damaged or destroyed two chairlifts.

It is now coming out of the shadows under new owners led by James Coleman of Durango, Colorado, whose partnership now directs Sipapu, Purgatory (near Durango, Colorado), Snowbowl (near Flagstaff, Arizona), and Pajarito. They are significantly improving its snowmaking capacity and plan to replace some of its oldest lifts.

It is something of a throwback ski area. Most days you ski onto the lifts. It still has some operational pit "privies," some two-people chairs, and a relaxed "our town hill" vibe. There are options for staying and dining in Los Alamos, but most skiers live here or visit from Albuquerque or Santa Fe for the day.

The only developed ski area in the Jemez Mountains, the summit of Pajarito provides extraordinary views. To the south is the range's dominant feature, the massive Valle Grande, the floor of an ancient, collapsed volcanic caldera, which you can see from a few viewpoints. To the east is the stunning Sangre de Cristo Range running northward past Taos and into Colorado. And to the north is nearby Tschicoma (or Chicoma or Santa Clara) Peak, the Jemez's highest point at 11,561 feet.

Mountain Highlights

Beginner Runs

It is a rare western ski area that has terrain that allows beginners to access the summit of their slopes and get down safely. Pajarito is one of those, with gentle runs curving off its wide flanks on long loops, bringing novices back to the base in one piece.

First-timers will need to build a few skills first on the dedicated beginner subarea right above the lodge. It is served by a rope tow and the beginner double chair.

But with some basics down, beginners can head up the Spruce chair and return via **East Run** (easiest), **Bonanza**, the long **Evershine Ridge**, or even **Lone Spruce** under the lift. Or, they can head up the Mother Chair and descend the area's west end on easygoing **Rim Run** to **West Road**, or Rim Run to **I Don't Care** to the uniquely named **Salamander Gully**.

Intermediate Runs

Much of Pajarito is an intermediate skier's delight. There are a few runs on the west end,

like **Why Not** and **One More Time**, and some in the area's midsection, like **Pussycat** and **Big Mother**. In addition, everything off the Townsight Chair is classified blue. Perhaps the best of this subarea is the run **Townsight**, dropping right under the chair.

Expert Runs

The toughest runs here are the area's so-called Fab Four—**Nuther Mother**, **Sidewinder**, **Breathless**, and **Precious**. They are never groomed and so develop monster moguls and include some quite steep pitches.

Powder

Since the ski area is closed normally on Mondays and Tuesdays, turning up here on a Wednesday after a storm cycle can provide some of the best powder skiing in the state. And, with its low skier numbers, it can also remain untracked for days. Once the open runs have been plundered, you can still find freshies in the trees (see below).

Bumps

See expert runs, above, for the toughest mogul runs. But less challenging bumps are also found from side to side on the mountain on various intermediate runs. Check the daily grooming report and avoid those runs if you are seeking moguls.

Trees

Volunteer and paid crews have been working hard over the years to thin the woods between runs and have created some really nice glens and glades here, even in sections not so designated. One named stash is **Porcupine Park** (on skier's left of Compromise). There is even some rare aspen tree skiing here, found in a pocket to skier's right at the top of Little Mother, below Oops.

Cruisers

Corresponding to its abundance of intermediate runs, Pajarito has many options for cruising. Check the grooming report for the day's best corduroy.

Terrain Parks

The ski area usually has two parks in operation. The beginner park, **Rail Yard**, with low-risk features, is located just above the base lodge. The second, named **Crazy Mother**, is a big step up, with significant jumps and more technical rails and features. Its jumps include dual takeoffs, allowing both intermediate and seasoned vets to pick their launch. It's found near the top of Big Mother.

Dining

The ski area has a modest cafeteria in the main lodge serving up burgers, sandwiches, and some hot dishes, with a large outdoor deck that is great in sunny weather. It opens for breakfast at 8 a.m. Brown baggers are welcome to grab a table.

Los Alamos is a fairly small town with limited options on dining. Here's the best of what it offers. For more choices, see the chapter on Ski Santa Fe.

The **Pajarito Brewpub and Grill** (614 Trinity Drive, 505-662-8877, www.pajaritobrewandpub.com) is a find, as well-done, progressive dining in Los Alamos is hard to come by. It features excellent salads, soups, made-to-order burgers, sandwiches, and appetizers like little neck clams and wings, plus 25 or more beers on tap and more in bottles, and a decent wine selection. **Cottonwood on the Greens** (4244 Diamond Drive, 505-662-0404, www.cottonwoodonthegreens.com) overlooks the local golf course and serves breakfast, lunch, and dinner. It too is surprisingly good. Dinner includes salmon, lamb, Italian dishes, made-to-order pizza, and many other choices.

Blue Window Bistro (813 Central Avenue, 505-662-6305, www.labluewindowbistro.com) has been in business since the 1980s, so that's a good sign of quality, due in part to its emphasis on fresh and local ingredients. It is open for lunch (soups, salads, sandwiches, burgers, and a few entrees) and dinner (pork tenderloin, seafood pasta, fish and chips, enchiladas, etc.), and serves beer and wine. **El Parasol** (1903 Central, 505-661-0303) is one of a handful of outlets of this locally owned New Mexican chain. It is open 7 a.m.–7 p.m. and serves up a scrumptious breakfast burrito. At lunch try the chicken guacamole tacos—some of the best in the state!

Pyramid Café (751 Central, 505-661-1717, www.pyramidcafesf.com), specializes in Mediterranean, Greek, and North African food, such as a tasty chicken tagin, couscous with organic lamb, falafel, spanakopita, and moussaka. Also has a beer and wine license. Open daily for lunch and dinner. **Bob's Bodacious BBQ** (3801 Arkansas Avenue, 505-662-4227, www.facebook.com/pages/Bobs-Bodacious-BBQ/120642654616527), is a bit off the beaten path but will reward you with excellent, reasonably priced BBQ. Try the melt-in-the-mouth ribs, gumbo, or brisket washed down by a good beer. It is closed, however, on weekends.

Origami (182 Central Park Square, 505-661-2592, www.facebook.com/pages/Origami/111812942184053), a Korean and sushi restaurant, is not what you'd expect to find in this town, but here it is and it's quite good. It is open Monday through Friday for lunch and dinner and dinner only on Saturdays; closed Sundays.

Pop in to **Smith's Marketplace** (751 Trinity Drive, 505-661-2757) for a yummy personal pizza, its gourmet grilled cheese counter, a salad, or rice/bean/meat bowls made to order, as well as the usual deli fair. And they have a beer/wine bar. If all you're seeking en route to or from the slopes is a good cup of coffee, there is also a **Starbucks** (1801 Central Avenue, 505-661-0100).

Lodging

There are no overnight accommodations at the ski area. Los Alamos, however, has a handful of options. Here are some suggestions. For more suggestions, see the chapter on Ski Santa Fe.

If you like bed-and-breakfasts, here are a few choices. Open since 1984, the longevity of **Margo's Bavarian Bed and Breakfast** (104 Monte Rey Drive North, 505-672-9274, www.Airbnb.com) says a lot. **Bandelier Bed and Breakfast** (135 La Senda Road, 505-672-9494) is another possibility.

The town also has a handful of chain hotels and motels. **Comfort Inn and Suites** (2455 Trinity, 505-661-1110) offers a free, hot breakfast and two nights of free lodging with the purchase of four adult lift tickets directly from the Inn. The **North Road Inn** (2127 North Road, 505-662-3678) offers the same lift ticket deal as the Comfort Inn. There is also a **Motel 6** (2175 Trinity Drive, 505-662-7211) with free Wi-Fi, and a **Holiday Inn Express** (60 Entrada Drive, 505-661-2646).

Nightlife

No one comes to Los Alamos for nightlife, but there are a few possibilities if you just seek some companionship and adult beverages. **Bathtub Row Brewing Co-op** (163 Central Park Square, 505-500-8381, www.bathtubrow brewing.coop) is open daily until 10 or 11 p.m.

In Addition to Downhill Skiing

Sitting on the edge of the Pajarito Plateau, huge canyons drop off the escarpment toward the Rio Grande thousands of feet below, providing hikers and other outdoor sporters with many other dry land activities, most of the year, in the Los Alamos area. A network of **hiking trails** laces the town, and short drives take you to tracks leading into **White Rock Canyon**.

Some 20 minutes away are the attractions of **Bandelier National Monument**, including 500-year-old Indian ruins, petroglyphs, an excellent interpretive center and museum, plus camping facilities.

About 40 minutes away is the **Valles Caldera National Preserve**, with its cross-country ski trails and other activities in winter (see Cross-Country Options section).

Right in town (hidden in a deep canyon but car accessible) is the **Los Alamos County Ice Rink** (4475 West Road, 505-662-4500). One of the state's few outdoor ice skating venues, it is open daily (conditions permitting), typically through mid-February. Rental skates and lessons are also offered.

Los Alamos was where the world's first nuclear bombs were developed and is home to several notable science and history museums. The **Bradbury Science Museum** documents the development of nuclear weapons through extensive exhibits, displays, film, and photos. The **Los Alamos Historical Museum** focuses more on the people involved and the prehistory of the area. Its **Fuller Lodge** dates back to the era of the Los Alamos Ranch School. Details on both can be found online. The **Manhattan Project National Historic Park** is in the process of being established in Los Alamos (and two other places nationwide), providing access to some of the research sites.

Natural hot springs flow in the Jemez Mountains, including **Spence Springs**, and an hour or so away are the funky, charming, old-school commercial pools, such as the **Jemez Bath House**, in the town of Jemez Springs.

Red River Ski Area

Address: Physical: 400 Pioneer Road, Red River, NM 87558; Mail: PO Box 990, Red River, NM 87558

Ski Report: 575-754-2223

Information: 800-331-7669, 575-754-2223

Websites: Ski area: www.redriverskiarea.com; Town of Red River: www.redriver.org; Red River Chamber of Commerce: www.redriver newmex.com

Facebook: RedRiverSkiArea

Twitter: @redriverskiarea

Instagram: @redriverskiarea

Operating Hours: 9 a.m.–4 p.m.

Season: Generally the day before Thanksgiving (weekends only until mid-December) through Easter

Mountain Profile

Base Elevation: 8,750 feet

Summit Elevation: hike-to 10,350 feet

Vertical Drop: 1,600 feet

Annual Snowfall: 214 inches

Area: 625 acres boundary (300 acres skiable)

Runs: 57 named

Longest Run: Cowpokes Cruise (2.1 miles)

Lifts: Seven (one quad chair, three triple chairs, one double chair, and two surface lifts)

Lift Capacity: 7,930 skiers per hour

Terrain Classification: Beginner: 32 percent; Intermediate: 38 percent; Expert: 30 percent

Terrain Parks: Three

Snowmaking: About 85 percent of the runs

Seasonal Visits: Number not available

Backcountry Access Policy: Closed boundary

Season Highlights: A USASA rail jam competition in early January; Winter Carnival with parades, ice carving, snowmobile races, fun ski races, and a wild "Skijoring" event with skiers towed behind horses over jumps down Main Street in mid to late January; Mardi Gras in the Mountains with costume contests, balls, live music, parades, and more in early February; the University of New Mexico Invitational slalom ski races in mid-February; and the end of season pond skim in late March. Many Saturday nights, and on Christmas Eve and New Year's Eve, the resort hosts a torchlight parade down The Face and fireworks.

Webcams: High-definition fixed camera with a view of Main Street and the ski area, plus controllable camera at three other locations

Amazing Facts: Brian "Cross Fire" Marshall set a world skiing record here in 1990, staying on his planks for an amazing 96 hours straight.

The Bottom Line: Red River, where "Mountain Meets Main Street," is a true ski town. Rustically Western, it is beloved by Texas visitors for its ambience and mostly tame terrain. But on a powder day you'll have entire runs to yourself and can walk or even ski to almost all lodging.

Getting Here

Driving

The ski area is located 170 miles north of Albuquerque, 110 miles north of Santa Fe, and 46 miles northeast of Taos, in the Carson National Forest.

If coming from the south, take NM 522 north from Taos 22 miles to Questa. In Questa, turn right (east) onto NM 38 and proceed about 13 miles to Red River.

If coming from the north, from Colorado, head south from La Jara on NM 522 to Questa, then turn left (east) onto NM 38.

If coming from the east (Texas, Oklahoma, or Kansas), head west on US 64 through Cimarron to Eagle Nest. In Eagle Nest, turn right (north) onto NM 38 and proceed over Bobcat Pass (9,280 feet) and into Red River.

Flying

The closest major airport is the Albuquerque Sunport, and commercial flights also land in Santa Fe daily. The drive from Albuquerque to Santa Fe town is one hour. You can rent a car in either Albuquerque (http://www.abq sunport.com/getting-around/rental-cars/)

or Santa Fe (I suggest four-wheel drive; visit https://santafe.org/Visiting_Santa_Fe/About_Santa_Fe/Getting_Around_Santa_Fe/).

Train and Bus Links

Amtrak stops in Lamy, 20 minutes south of Santa Fe.

There is also a commuter rail service, the **Rail Runner** (www.nmrailrunner.com), which runs multiple times a day from Albuquerque to the downtown Santa Fe Depot. It includes a bus link in Albuquerque to the airport.

The North Central Regional Transportation District (i.e., the **Blue Bus**) has service between the Santa Fe Depot and Red River, via Taos and Questa. There are eight trips a day between Questa and Red River. For more information and a schedule, call 866-206-0754 or visit www.RideTheBlueBus.com.

Within town, a free **trolley** cruises up and down Main Street and to the ski area base during the day, making it a breeze to get around. It runs an extended schedule during holidays.

Maps

A good map of the area showing accommodations and other landmarks can be found at http://www.red-river-nm.com/custimages/RRRE-InTownMap-Aug11.pdf.

Services

Lift Tickets

Adult full day at least $68, half day at least $53; teens (13–19), full day at least $62, half day at least $48; juniors (4–12), full day at least $52, half day at least $38; seniors (65–69), full day at least $52, half day at least $38; free for children 3 and younger and seniors 70 and older. Group rates for 20 or more skiers and other discounts available; call or visit website. Ticket-only kiosks are found at the Main Chalet and the bottom of the Platinum and Copper chairs.

Rentals

The resort-based rental shop at the Main Chalet opens at 7:30 a.m. Its regular rental skis, boots, and poles run at least $28 for adults (ages 18–64) and $22 for juniors; snowboards run at least $33 for adults and juniors. They also rent snow blades: at least $26 for adults and $20 for juniors. The shop also carries a small selection of premier demo skis, and helmets. Reservations can be made online (no less than 72 hours in advance). You can pick up gear after 2 p.m. the day prior to your outing to save time the next morning.

There are also numerous shops in town that rent gear. These include **Sitzmark Sports** (416 West Main Street, 575-754-2525, 800-843-7547, www.sitzmarknm.com), a long-standing facility with premier skis and snowboards, plus rental snowshoes, ski blades, and apparel; **Wild Bill's Ski and Snowboard Shop** (325 West Main Street, 575-754-2428, www.wild billski.com); and **All Season Sports** (600 West Main Street, 575-754-2308, 800-686-3485, www.allseasonsrrnm.com), with high-performance rentals plus sales of top apparel brands.

Tuning Shop

Anything from a complete tune-up to a quick edge job or waxing can be done here. Located in the rental shop at the base.

Retail Shops

The **Fanny Pack**, on the ground level of the Main Chalet, is open 8 a.m.–4 p.m. Many other shops selling everything from skiwear to car batteries are just a short walk from the base. There is also a large grocery store, **Der Markt** (307 West Main Street, 575-754-2974), open daily; it also carries beer, wine, and spirits.

Ski School

The **Youth Ski Center** (located right next to the Main Chalet, 575-754-2223) provides lessons, group or private, to skiers ages 4–12 and to snowboarders ages 6–12. It also offers private lessons only for three-year-olds. Lesson packages include two two-hour group lessons, lift ticket, and rental equipment, with optional lunch. With lunch, it costs at least $136. A half-day package is at least $115. A single two-hour lesson runs at least $65. Lessons for riding in the terrain park can also be provided. The program sells out during peak periods, so be sure to make reservations.

For adults (ages 20–64), a three-hour group beginner session runs at least $114, for teens at least $109, and seniors at least $102. Lessons for returning skiers cost slightly more, and snowboarding lessons cost a bit more than ski lessons.

One-hour private lessons run at least $75 for the first person and $45 for additional students. Reservations are required (575-754-2223, ext. 601).

Adaptive Ski Program

Limited, with 14-day advance request

Childcare

Buckaroo Day Care is located in the upper-level Main Chalet. It operates 8:30 a.m.–4:30 p.m. and accepts children ages 6 months–4 years. A full day costs at least $85 and a half day at least $55. Reservations are not required, but there's a limit on attendance. Call 575-754-2223 for details.

Lockers

Rentals are available in the lift house and the Main Chalet.

Cell Phone Service

Excellent

First Aid

Three locations: The Chalet (in main base complex), the Lift House (at base of Platinum chair, 200A Pioneer Road), and the top of the Platinum and Copper chairs (575-754-2333). Also operating out of the lift house is **UltiMed**, a full-service urgent care center (575-754-1773). Another option is the **Red River Medical Center** (421 East Main Street, 575-754-6330, www.redrivermedicalcare.com), which serves walk-ins and minor emergency visits.

Background

Pop quiz: What New Mexico locale is nicknamed Ski Town of the Southwest? If you guessed Taos Ski Valley, you'd be wrong. It is, at most, a village. For a real town, where the

ski lifts ascend right from the streets and where you can stroll the sidewalks for après-ski dining or visit an infamous country saloon, drop in on the town of Red River and its street-side ski area.

Its relatively easygoing slopes, sprinkled with a handful of steep shots, have been attracting predominantly Texas skiers and families since its opening in 1959. If God had given Texas and Oklahoma a mountain resort, it would be named Red River. Part of that is due to geography and part to intention. The town is the closest mountain resort to northern Texas and Oklahoma, and long ago their residents discovered its winter, and summer, attractions. The town realized it had a solid clientele base and determined to make them feel at home. Thus, Red River is something of a fantasy, an anachronistic model of what a "Western" town is supposed to be. Its streets are called trails, dogs wander in and out of

honky-tonks, and storefronts of timber and clapboard facades is the principle architectural motif, but the cowboy hats are a way of life, not a fashion statement.

A visit here is always a refreshing experience that harkens back to a simpler era in skiing. And because its skiers and boarders are mostly beginner and intermediates, in stormy weather you can spend a full day skiing untracked powder. For some visitors, snow is a rarity: there are lots of snowball fights and snowmen built, and one story relates that during a two-inch-an-hour snowfall, a tourist excitedly asked, "Is this man-made or natural?"

Linton Judycki, deputy general manager of the ski area along with Walt Foley, grew up here. Judycki once told me, "I skied on the mountain almost every day. When I was in second or third grade I got an award for being the kid who wore their ski pants the most to school. When we were let out, I could get in an hour or so on the mountain." His father, Drew Judycki, was the general manager of the ski area at the time, and then bought the operation in the late 1980s.

Says Foley, "It's a quaint, rustic little place, with a great clientele. Many are generational skiers. We always get comments like, 'My grandfather took me here and now I'm here with my kids.'"

Red River goes out of its way to amuse children. On the top of the mountain you'll find Moon Star Mining Camp, which is a maze of narrow dipsy-doodle trails pocketed with wooden cutouts of animals, an Indian village, miners' cabins, and other whimsical stuff.

Red River's first attempt at a ski area came in 1940, when a rope tow was erected. It was shut down in December 1941, the day after Pearl Harbor was attacked. In 1959, Oklahoman Stokes Bolton decided he'd like to have a place to re-create in winter and built the first chairlift, a poma lift, and a rope tow.

The community's roots extend to the 1860s, with gold, silver, and copper mines being worked throughout the region, but it was incorporated as a town in 1895. In 1905 it had a population of some 3,000 souls. Today it has about 500 year-round residents. Its former "ambassador-at-large," Wally Dobbs, who passed away in 2015 after being inducted into the New Mexico Ski Hall of Fame, once told me, "The thing about Red River is that after you've been here three days, you're a native." So if you want to feel like a local, simply settle in for a bit and see if you don't start feeling at home in New Mexico's friendliest ski town.

Mountain Highlights

A few navigational tips: the easiest way to get from the primary base area—where the Main Chalet, ski school, rentals, and other services are located—to the rest of the mountain is to take the Gold chair up the beginner slope and then stay to skier's right to get on Platinum Way.

From the top of the Platinum or Copper chairs to reach Cat Skinner and its neighboring expert runs, or to reach the Silver chair

runs, ski off the back side to the Green chair and ride it up.

Beginner Runs

Red River introduces a lot of people to skiing and has good terrain to do so. The flattest slopes, including **Gold Rush**, are found right next to and above the Main Chalet. This subarea is served by a short chairlift, the Gold, and two magic carpet lifts.

Once you have mastered the basics, you can ride either the Platinum or Copper chairs to the summit and ski into the back side runs served by the new Emerald chair in the popular **Moon Star Mining Camp** sector. These include **Moon Shadow**, **Sunnyside**, and **Cow Pattie Lane**, **Moon Star**, and **Golden Treasure**. This is a very popular area for novices, as the runs are easygoing, and, as it faces east, it also warms up here sooner than other parts of the mountain, making it a pleasant destination. A beginner trail, **Cow Poke's Cruise** (to Lariat) at the bottom of the Emerald chair wraps around the mountain, bringing you back around to the front side and eventually to Lariat and access to the base.

Intermediate Runs

A nice stash of intermediate terrain is found off the Silver chair, including **Silverado**, **Lucky Strike**, and **True Grit**. All of the runs noted in the Cruisers section are also fine intermediate offerings, as are the runs served by the Emerald chair (see section above).

Expert Runs

For a place beloved by "flatlanders," Red River has a surprisingly large selection of expert runs when they all open. A classic off the top is **Cat Skinner**, which has some really steep pitches. I recall my daughter, Isabel, in tears on it, bogged down at the top of one section. Off it, drop into **Airplane** and **Landing Strip** and then cut back to the Platinum chair on Platinum Way.

To skier's left of Cat Skinner is **Bad Medicine**, another really precipitous pitch, which you can link to **Powder Keg** or **Gulch**, both very narrow and sheer. Also off the Platinum chair seek out the short but well-named **Mine Shaft** and **Dropout**.

Miners Alley, **Tailings**, and testy pitches

under the Copper chair are super steep, if short. Perhaps the sheerest drop of all is **Linton's Leap**, especially its top half. It seems that with a good spring you might end up downtown on Main Street!

Powder

Few skiers or boarders here like powder, so if you do you're golden, especially during a storm cycle. During or after a storm, almost any expert run and the edges of most intermediate runs become an endless descent in fluff, run after run after run after run. It can get really deep on the back side, off the Silver chair, on the runs **Rainbow's End** and **Wild Turkey**.

Bumps

Most of the expert runs go ungroomed, so seek those out to bang bumps. **Maverick** always has a gut that is heavily moguled, and **Rainbow's End** is a knee burner.

Trees

While not a significant interest for most people here, Red River has created some really nice tree skiing in recent years. This includes the dedicated glade, **Sluice Box Glade** (to skier's left of **Dropout**). And carefully poking around will reveal other small pockets in the woods. On a snow day, you can ski low-angle lines among aspens between the top of the Silver chair and the bottom of the Green chair, an unusual treat in New Mexico.

Cruisers

The most popular avenue down-the-front face is linking up **Main Street** or **Kit Carson**, off either the Platinum or Copper chairs, to **Broadway**, the aptly named run that rolls back to the base. **Boomtown** is also a blast to bomb down, as is **Downtown**.

Ute Chute is fairly steep but always nicely groomed for laying down some fast GS turns. The Face, right at the bottom of the Platinum chair, is always beautifully groomed and fairly steep, allowing you to really carve away for the folks sitting on the balcony of the Lift House.

Terrain Parks

Novice tricksters should head to the beginner slope at the base and its **Pot o' Gold Park**. A far more challenging park, **Hollywood**, is located under the Platinum chair. It usually features 35 rails and boxes, plus jumps from 25 to 40 feet. A midway unloading station provides great access for laps.

Dining

On the Mountain

Most folks head to the base area's **Main Chalet Cafeteria and Grill** for lunch. Good, solid meals range from grilled cheese sandwiches to barbecue, green chile stew, and loaded baked potatoes. Open at 7:30 a.m., it's also popular for breakfast and has terrific views of the runs above through its two-story windows or off its large deck.

The **Lift House Grill** (at the bottom of the Platinum chair, 575-754-2223) is a classic old ski bar and restaurant where many a raging party went off in the 1970s. Recently remodeled and expanded, it serves excellent burgers, sandwiches, wings, salads, and such. Its large deck is the place to watch torchlight parades and fireworks, or catch some rays on a spring day.

At the summit, atop the Platinum and Copper chairs, is the **Ski Tip** (575-754-6108), with basic grub, along with beer and wine. In good weather, its outdoor deck provides wonderful views.

And, for lunch, Main Street and its many restaurants are just a short walk from the lifts (see below).

In Town

On weekends and holidays, it's wise to call ahead and make reservations for dinner, if possible, as an hour wait is not uncommon in Red River during peak periods.

One of the oldest and best places to have lunch or dinner is **Texas Red's Steakhouse** (400 East Main Street, 575-754-2922, www. texasredssteakhouse.com). Its fireplace, wood paneling, and attached bar, the **Lost Love Saloon**, have an old-time charm, and the roast beef and T-bones are deservedly famous.

Sundance (401 High Street, 575-754-2971, www.facebook.com/Sundance-Restaurant-120500607989247), opened in 1974, is the place to go for good New Mexican fare—chile rellenos, enchiladas, carne adovada, and so forth, plus steaks and tamer fare. Try the wine margaritas for something different, or stick to beer and wine. Open for dinner only.

Capo's (Pioneer Road at base of Platinum chair, 575-754-6297, www.caposredriver.com),

established in 1995, is another of the better places to eat, featuring Italian food, wine, and beer. A good choice is one of the homemade pizzas.

Also very close to the base lifts and Main Chalet is **Black Diamond Grill** (305 Pioneer Road, 575-754-9950), with daily specials, burgers, Texas BBQ, beer, wine, and a daily happy hour for après-ski.

Brett's Bistro (201 W. Main Street, 575-754-9959) is known for its steaks, seafood, and trout, plus daily specials, for both lunch and dinner. It also serves wine and beer and takes reservations.

For an adventurous dinner, reserve a spot on the **Snow Coach Tours** (575-754-2223, ext. 3). A snowcat will haul you up the mountain to dine in the Ski Tip at an elevation of 10,350 feet, where you will enjoy a three-course meal with your choice of steak with garlic herb compound butter, Chilean sea bass in mushroom garlic white wine sauce, or deep-fried herbed game hen, and a variety of desserts. It runs twice a night almost every night. Reservations are required.

Lodging

With some 6,000 pillows in town, one can choose from a wide range of accommodations in Red River, from inexpensive motels and tiny log cabins to hotels and luxury condos.

A great middle ground is the **Auslander Condominiums** (303 Pioneer Road, 800-753-2311, www.auslandercondominiums.biz). Just a few minutes' walk from the chairlifts, very clean units include a full kitchen, nice living rooms, free Wi-Fi, lots of storage space, and a hot tub and sauna for relaxing after a day on the slopes.

The **Alpine Lodge** (417 Main Street, 800-252-2333) is a classic-looking Swiss inn just a few blocks from the ski area. It features two hot tubs and a dry sauna, and some units have kitchens and wood fireplaces.

The **Best Western River's Edge Lodge** (301 West River Street, 877-600-9990) is also very close to the chairlifts and offers a free hot breakfast and a guest laundry.

Lifts West Condominium Hotel (201 West Main Street, 800-221-1859, www.liftswest.

com) is another convenient location and has full kitchens, free Wi-Fi, satellite TV, a heated pool, and covered parking.

Nightlife

Something else not to be missed here is a stop into one of the town's two classic watering holes, the **Motherlode** (406 Main Street, 575-754-6280,www.facebook.com/motherlode-saloon-red-river-nm-183525161246) and **Bull o' the Woods** (401 Main Street, 575-754-2593, www.bullowoods.com)—located conveniently across East Main Street from each other. The Motherlode opened in 1936 and saw such stars as Jerry Jeff Walker and other Austin bands tear it up in the 1970s and '80s. Both host live local and touring bands every weekend night, so be sure to plan for a little boot scootin'. Both have pool tables and draw lively crowds.

In Addition to Skiing

Tubing

The ski area offers tubing with a magic carpet lift on the slope just to the side of the Main Chalet after 4 p.m. A limited number of tickets are sold, beginning at 7:30 a.m. daily.

Snowmobiling

Red River is one of New Mexico's centers of snowmobile culture (along with Chama, Angel Fire, and Ruidoso). Businesses offer guided tours ranging from one and a half hours to daylong outings for solo or dual riders, operational instruction, and appropriate clothing and helmets. Options include **Bobcat Pass Wilderness Adventures** (operating atop Bobcat Pass on NM 38, office at 200 West Main Street, 575-754-2769, www.bobcatpass.com); **Red River Sled Shed** (616 West Main Street, 800-395-0121, www.redriversledshed.com), the town's oldest such operation; and **Red River Offroad** (500 East Main Street, 575-754-6335).

Snowshoeing

There are a handful of trails leading into the canyons flanking the main valley, including **Mallette**, **Bitter Creek**, **Placer Creek**, and **Pioneer Creek**. Several shops in town rent shoes and poles.

Cross-Country Skiing

The state's only developed, commercial cross-country operation, **Enchanted Forest Cross County and Snowshoe Area**, is located just three and a half miles from town. There are also numerous hiking trails (see above) that double in winter as cross-country paths. Contact the district forest service office for information. Also see part 2, "Cross-Country Options," for additional options.

Sandia Peak

Address: Physical: Mile marker 6, Crest Scenic Byway / NM 536, Sandia Park, NM 87047; Mail: 10 Tramway Loop NE, Albuquerque, NM 87122

Ski Report: 505-857-8977

Information: 505-242-9052

Websites: www.sandiapeak.com, www.visitalbuquerque.org

Facebook: Sandia Peak

Twitter: @sandiapeak

Instagram: @sandiapeak

Operating Hours: 9 a.m.–4 p.m., days vary throughout season but generally Fridays–Sundays and holidays

Season: Generally mid-December through mid-March

Mountain Profile

Base Elevation: 8,678 feet

Summit Elevation: hike-to 10,378 feet; lift-served 10,350 feet

Vertical Drop: 1,700 feet

Annual Snowfall: 125 inches

Area: 200 acres

Runs: 38 named

Longest Run: Cibola (2.5 miles)

Lifts: Five (four double chairs and one surface)

Lift Capacity: 4,500 skiers per hour

Terrain Classification: Beginner: 35 percent; Intermediate: 55 percent; Expert: 10 percent

Terrain Parks: One

Snowmaking: About 15 percent of the runs

Seasonal Visits: 18,764 skiers per year

Backcountry Access Policy: Open

Season Highlights: The KOAT-TV Learn a Winter Sport program, held every January for skiers and snowboarders ages 7–12, has become the ski area's most prominent annual event, with steep discounts on rentals, lift tickets, and lessons.

Webcams: One, fixed atop Chair 1

Amazing Facts: One of the oldest ski areas in the West, Sandia Peak's predecessor area, La Madera, was launched in 1936. Today it is reached directly from Albuquerque via a world engineering marvel, the Sandia Peak Tramway.

The Bottom Line: With perhaps the fastest access to skiing of any major city in the nation, via the spectacular Sandia Peak Tramway, this small-scale, modestly pitched mountain is a great, quick getaway, especially nice on a powder day or under the spring sun. With stupendous views from the top, its terrain calls out to intermediates and beginners but can satisfy almost all tastes.

Getting Here

Driving

The ski area is located just east of Albuquerque in the Cibola National Forest unit of the Sandia Mountains.

One can drive to the Sandia Peak Tramway base station within the city limits, on its far east edge just off Tramway Boulevard, and quickly access the ski area this way. (See tram details below.)

Or, you can drive east out of Albuquerque on I-40 and take exit 175 at Tijeras onto NM 14 North. Proceed through the village of Cedar Crest and turn left onto NM 536. This two-lane road, a National Scenic Byway, climbs fairly steeply (four-wheel drive suggested during storms) for six miles to the ski area base. The drive takes 45–60 minutes from town.

If coming from Santa Fe, either drive to the tram station or drive south on NM 14 to Cedar Crest and turn right onto NM 536.

Sandia Peak Tramway

A truly impressive engineering feat, it climbs 2.7 miles and nearly 4,000 vertical feet in 15 minutes, from the cactus and yucca of its base station at an elevation of 6,559 feet to the snow-crusted pines at 10,378 feet, providing skiers with quick and easy access to the goods.

However, you must have all needed equipment with you to ride the tram, as the ski area's rental shop is located at the base of the mountain and the tram debarks at the summit.

The tram operates daily in winter 9 a.m.– 8 p.m., except on Tuesdays when it runs 5 p.m. – 8 p.m. only. A round-trip adult ticket costs at least $15 when purchased with a full-day lift ticket, or at least $25 otherwise. The tram base station is located at 30 Tramway Road. To get there from I-40, take exit 167 (Tramway Boulevard / NM 556) and head north about nine miles to Tramway Road. Turn right and proceed to the terminal. To get there from I-25, take exit 234 (NM 556) east six miles. Turn left onto Tramway Road and proceed to the terminal. For details, call 505-856-7325 or visit www.sandiapeak.com.

The tram center is also home to the small **New Mexico Ski Hall of Fame and Museum**. It is a must-see for anyone interested in the history of skiing in this "desert" state. Admission is free.

Flying

The closest major airport is the Albuquerque Sunport. You can rent a car in Albuquerque (http://www.abqsunport.com/getting-around/rental-cars/).

Train and Bus Links

Amtrak stops in Albuquerque. There is no bus service to the ski area.

Services

Lift Tickets

Adult all-day lift tickets cost at least $55, half day at least $40; students (13–23) full day at least $45, half day at least $35; children (12 and under) all day at least $40, half day at least $30; seniors (62–71), full day at least $45. Active-duty military full day costs at least $40. Children under 46 inches (in boots) are free, as are super seniors over 72 years of age. Groups of 15 or more can qualify for reduced rates. Call 505-856-6419 for details.

The best option for raw beginners, either ski-ers or boarders, is a combined all-day beginner lift ticket, including rentals and four hours of lessons, which costs at least $80. A similar deal exists for people who've mastered the basics. It includes an all-day lift pass and two hours of instruction, and it costs at least $90.

A combined all-day lift ticket and tram pass costs at least $65; tram pass and a half-day lift ticket costs at least $50. Season passes and other discounts are available.

Rentals

The ski area's base rental shop opens at 8:15 a.m. Its regular rental skis, boots, and poles for adults and teens cost at least $23, and for kids 6 and under at least $18. Snowboard rentals run at least $28 and at least $38 with boots. Helmets cost at least $12.

The resort also offers combined rental, lift ticket, and instruction deals—see above.

You can fill out online forms for rentals and lessons in advance and bring them with you to speed up the registration process.

IN ALBUQUERQUE

Tuning

Ski tuning services are not done at the ski area (see listing above for that).

Retail Shops

The **Sandia Peak Sports Shop** in the base area has a good selection of essentials and accessories, including logo gear.

Ski School

Sandia provides ski and snowboard lessons to anyone from first-timers to experts. A two-hour group session costs at least $40. A full-day group lesson runs at least $60. A one-hour private lesson runs at least $65 (and $35 per additional person).

Adaptive Ski Program

Sandia Peak serves skiers and boarders with physical and mental challenges, and provides private lessons, equipment rentals, and lessons at a nominal fee. For reservations or details, call 505-995-9858 or visit www.adaptivesports program.org.

Childcare

Cubby Corner, for kids ages 4–6, provides a variety of services, including instruction and rentals, if needed. It runs 10 a.m.–12 p.m. and 1 p.m.–3 p.m. Half day, without rental gear, costs at least $50 and at least $72 with rentals; a combined morning and afternoon session costs at least $72 without rentals and at least $90 with rentals.

Mountain Tours

None

Lockers

Found at the upper terminal of the tram and in the base area lodge

Cell Phone Service

Spotty

First Aid

There are ski patrol centers at both the top and the bottom of the ski area. Call through the main number.

Background

Sandia Peak is, surprisingly, the oldest of New Mexico's ski areas, and one of the oldest in the West. Its first runs were cut and skied on in 1936, and its first lift—a rope tow—was installed in 1937, operating as La Madera Ski Area. The ski area grew out of an informal club of residents who took up skiing.

Leading the charge was young Robert Nordhaus, who was born in Las Vegas, New Mexico, and educated at Yale, and his wife, Virginia. Pamela Salmon, in her book *Sandia Peak: A History of the Sandia Peak Tramway and Ski Area*, says of Nordhaus, "Almost singlehandedly for decades he championed a sport almost no one thought could exist in New Mexico. . . . Bob conceived, organized, developed, financed and found financing for, and encouraged participation in, the establishment and growth of skiing in the Sandia Mountains east of Albuquerque." They warmed themselves in tents and ate outdoors around fires. World War II interrupted the nascent ski area's development, with Nordhaus joining the famed 10th Mountain Division, which specialized in on-snow combat.

Working alongside him was Pete Totemoff, an Aleut Indian from Alaska who did

everything from teaching skiing to splicing cable, running the sawmill, and dynamiting stumps. In 1946 they were joined by Buzz Bainbridge, who first arrived in the region as a salesman for Northland skis. Buzz and his wife, Jean, served as managers at La Madera for a few years and played a significant role in developing skiing above Santa Fe, as well as launching Arizona Snowbowl near Flagstaff, Arizona.

Ben Abruzzo and his wife, Pat, arrived in Albuquerque in 1952 and got stuck in the mud on the ski area road on their first visit, but they fell in love with it all. Abruzzo became manager in 1957 and bought half of the ownership from Nordhaus in 1958.

In 1966, at a then-daunting cost of $2 million, a 60-passenger jig-back tramway was strung up the jagged 4,000-foot-high west face of the Sandias, providing a direct link between the urban foothills and the grand mountain crest where the ski area chairs also top out. It was, and is, an engineering marvel, with breathtaking views, passage over deep canyons and across cliff faces, and the third-largest span between towers of any tram in the world. It rises through four of earth's seven life zones. The project was overseen by Nordhaus and Abruzzo. Over the years Abruzzo became executive vice president and general manager, with Nordhaus remaining as president, until 1971 when Abruzzo assumed that role as well. His family continues to operate it today, with their father lost in a plane accident in February 1985. That disaster happened just three months after the family had bought the Santa Fe Ski Basin, a moment of joy turned to ashes. Responsibility for running both areas fell to son Louis (then age 29) and younger brothers Benny and Richard.

Nordhaus passed away in 2007, after having been picked as one of the 16 Founders of Skiing USA by *Ski* and *Skiing* magazines.

Changes continue on the mountain. The old Summit House, remodeled in the 1980s into the restaurant and bar High Finance, is being completely rebuilt. It is expected to reopen in August 2018. It appears that half of New Mexico can be seen from its floor-to-ceiling windows facing west on the summit rim. Also forthcoming is the new Mountain Coaster (see In Addition to Downhill Skiing section).

The city also has one option for rentals, with a next-morning return policy. **Sport Systems** (6915 Montgomery Boulevard NE, 505-837-9400) rents basic boards, boots, skis and poles plus demo lines, backcountry and cross-country gear, snowshoes, and clothing, and it has a full-service tuning shop.

It was rough but fun. In the early 1960s, I recall being dragged through the brush lining a diabolical T-bar tow that dumped many riders. It had been installed in 1946, as the longest in the nation, and was still operating in the early 1960s. Thankfully, in 1963 a 7,500-foot double Stadeli chair was opened, running from the base to the rim in one shot. Chair 1 still stands today. We dried off and warmed up around a fireplace in a timber lodge built by the Civilian Conservation Corps. More runs were opened and the place was packed on weekends.

That same year, a Summit House restaurant, designed by Max Flatow, was added, which was a wonderful thing, even though running it was hell—everything had to be carried up on the double chair. I remember riding up that chair once on a dark December afternoon with my younger friend John Allen, into a wind blowing over the rim and right down the chair line, as it was known to do. He was crying and I was barely functioning. We got into the Summit House and thawed out with some french fries eaten around the fireplace.

Mountain Highlights

Beginner Runs

The primary beginner terrain is found at the base of the area, just above the Day Lodge. A beginner chair rises 300 vertical feet over a

span of 1,500 feet, providing access to a gentle, wide slope. To one side is a surface Mitey Mite lift for small kids.

Sandia is also one of those rare ski areas where beginners can ski from the summit down. **Fred's Run** (accessed via Chairs 1, 2, or 3) to **Hups** provides a nice meandering route from the top back to the base. **Cibola**, which forks off of Fred's Run, offers another beginner run down to the base.

Intermediate Runs

Intermediates can have a memorable day here since a large part of the mountain is available to them, with runs scattered from one side to the other. The most obvious one is the broad, fall-line run **Exhibition**, which unspools down the mountain under Chair 1. Running parallel to it under Chair 3 is **Prohibition**, and next to it are **Sandia** and **Aspen**. On the far north edge is **Double Eagle**. Most funnel into **Lower Slalom** and back to the base.

Expert Runs

The expert runs here are really just short, steep pitches. But when we were young, it seemed the definition of insanity to ski **Suicide**, and almost equally precipitous are **Little Suicide**,

Greg's, and **Burn**. The longest and most sustained run on the mountain is **Diablo**.

Powder

With its largely beginner and intermediate customer base, this can be a surprisingly delightful place to turn up on a powder day, especially on a Friday after snow may have built up. Most skiers will stick to the groomed slopes, and you will have much of the mountain to yourself.

Guy Jackson, who raced on the University of New Mexico ski team under coach George Brooks, has been skiing at Sandia and its predecessor, La Madera, for more than five decades. He notes, "After a considerable storm, **Do-Drop-In**, **Slalom**, **Burn**, and **Suicide** are the choice steeper runs that are all sought after for first tracks. **Diablo** is another favorite after a new snow, which challenges a skier to make quick slalom turns through the narrow trail that was a platter pull lift alignment in the late fifties / early sixties."

Bumps

Once the freshies are skied out, **Do-Drop-In**, **Slalom**, **Burn**, and **Suicide** are transformed into great bump runs, with Suicide being the most challenging with the steepest terrain.

Trees

There is a small pocket, **Aspen Glade**, near the top between Sandia and Aspen that provides some fine tree skiing after a storm. In a good year, one can also venture into other tree islands between runs, where caredful poking around will reward you with some turns.

Cruisers

Much of Sandia's terrain is perfect for cruising—fairly wide, modestly pitched runs that are finely manicured, which makes almost all of the mountain absolutely fantastic for cruising. Among the finest is Exhibition, which affords awesome views through your ski tips of the vast, high plains running east toward Texas.

"Double Eagle and Exhibition are my favorites because of the openness and the varied terrain of these high-speed cruisers," says Sandia veteran Guy Jackson.

He elaborates, "The lower section of **Double Eagle** narrows a bit in a gully-shaped drainage that allows a skier to set up and transition into the steep headwall where the trail intersects with the lower portion of Diablo. This makes for a perfect arena to lay down some giant slalom turns at speed, followed by a long compression at **Silver Arrow** and into the Race Arena for an accomplished finish. Double Eagle was once used for an NCAA race in the early eighties and Silver Arrow was the race hill during the La Madera days.

"**Exhibition** has its own interesting terrain features as it transitions into a steeper headwall section that finishes off with a big right footer that intersects with the lower section of Aspen Bowl. Lower Exhibition gives way to Slalom, which is one of the steepest headwalls of the mountain."

Terrain Parks

There is a small terrain park, the **Scrapyard**, with a handful of fun boxes and rails. It is located in the base area served by Chair 4 and is open based on snow conditions.

Dining

On the Mountain

In the base area, on the upper level of the Day Lodge, is the **Double Eagle II Café**. It opens at 8:30 a.m. for breakfast and again for lunch. Breakfast options include burritos, hot and cold cereal, pastries, yogurt, and fruit. Lunch includes burgers, hot dogs, grilled chicken sandwiches, quesadillas, Frito pie, salads, and assorted sides and desserts.

At the summit, just above Chairs 1, 2, and 3, is **High Finance Restaurant** (505-243-9742, though name and contact details may change after this book goes to print). Only a few steps from the top Sandia Peak Tramway station, it also appeals to non-skiers and is open for dinner and lunch. It presents tremendous views in all directions and enjoys full bar service with locally crafted beer. Closed for the 2017–2018 season while its previous incarnation is torn down and completely rebuilt, its food focuses on high-quality, hand-cut meats and fish from the show grill and nightly specials. The bar/bistro offers casual dining with its own menu. A new elevator eliminates the trudge up numerous flights of stairs from the chairlifts, and makes the facility ADA compliant.

There is also a good restaurant, **Sandiago's** (40 Tramway Road, 505-856-6692), located in the tram base station in Albuquerque, which is open for lunch and dinner with a full bar. It specializes in New Mexican fare, dishes like roasted green chile stew, carne adovada, and blue corn enchiladas, plus specialties such as steak tampiqueña, grilled portabella, and fresh mahimahi. It is closed for lunch on Tuesdays.

In Town

Albuquerque is becoming a foodie town, with many interesting and excellent restaurants popping up.

Seasons Rotisserie and Grill (2031 Mountain Road, 505-766-5100, www.seasonsabq.com) is one of the city's most consistently good places to dine, with excellent service and food. Opened in 1996 on the north side of Old Town, it serves up classics like prime rib, grilled center-cut sirloin, and oak-fired jumbo shrimp, as well as healthy and inventive salads, soups, appetizers, and other entrees.

Zinc Wine Bar and Bistro (3009 Central Avenue, 505-254-9462, www.zincabq.com), a sister establishment to Seasons, provides imaginative, fresh, and well-prepared dishes across a broad spectrum. It has a full bar and excellent service.

The **Artichoke Café** (424 Central Avenue, 505-243-0200, www.artichokecafe.com) is one of the oldest fine-dining outposts in the city, focusing on fresh, local, and seasonal foods prepared with French craftsmanship and paired with a large wine list. Open daily for lunch and dinner, with a special bar menu.

One of the newer arrivals to the finer side of dining is **Frenchish** (3509 Central Avenue NE, 505-433-5911, www.frenchish.com), under the capable hand of chef-owner Jennifer James, who has established a thriving career based on fresh and organic foods imaginatively prepared.

For Italian, try **Scalo Northern Italian Grill** (3500 Central Avenue, 505-255-8781, www.scalonobhill.com), which has stood the test of time with its consistently good food and sharp service. It has a large antipasti menu, wood-fired pizza, and a great selection of pasta and meat dishes. With a full bar and a special happy hour menu, it's very popular; reservations are recommended.

Many people come to New Mexico to sample its best-in-nation "Mexican" food, and Albuquerque is bursting with options. Some of the best include **El Pinto** (on the north edge of the city at 10500 4th Street NW, 505-898-1771, www.elpinto.com), a bit pricey but always good; either of the affordable **Monroe's** restaurants (www.monroeschile.com); any of the three **Garcia's Kitchen** locations (www.garciaskitchen.com); or **Mary and Tito's** (2711 4th Street NW, 505-344-6266, www.facebook.com/Mary-Titos-285797620198)

Also in the North Valley, but worth the drive, is **Farm and Table** (8917 4th Street NW, 505-503-7124, www.farmandtablenm.com), which specializes in the freshest seasonal ingredients—many harvested right from their own on-site fields. It is open just for dinner Wednesday through Saturday, and for brunch on Saturday and Sunday.

Other places I can recommend include the affordable **Flying Star** establishments (great for breakfast and lunch), the healthy and tasty **Vinaigrette**, the romantic Old Town enclaves of **Michelle's Kitchen** (French) and **Antiquity Restaurant**, the **Nob Hill Bar and Grill** in midtown, the **Rancher's Club** (for meat eaters), **High Noon** (in Old Town), and **Bien Shur** (with awesome views of the Sandia mountains).

Lodging

There are no on-site overnight accommodations at the ski area, but Albuquerque has the largest bed base in the state, with a complete range of options from bed-and-breakfasts to cheap motels and luxury digs.

If money is no object, spend a night or three at **Los Poblanos** (4803 Rio Grande Boulevard NW, 866-344-9297, www.lospoblanos.com), a historic property set on 25 acres in the heart of a former farming district with plentiful trees, fields, and pastures. Each impeccably finished room has a fireplace; the main structure is the former home of a state governor, filled with fine furniture and great spaces. The Territorial-style home was designed by one of New Mexico's most renowned architects and exudes a rare calm, charm, and style. Its kitchen is one of the best in the state, featuring organic and local produce, meats, and breads, Wednesdays through Sundays.

A super-convenient place to stay if skiing Sandia Peak, **Sandia Resort and Casino** (30 Rainbow Road NE, 505-796-7500, www.sandiacasino.com) is just five minutes from the tramway and on the north edge of the city, making trips to Santa Fe and Taos that much easier. Perhaps the most attractive of all the Indian-run casinos in the state, it includes a full-service hotel, award-winning 18-hole golf course, a spa, restaurants, nightclubs, and, of course, a full range of gaming options in its 140,000-square-foot casino.

The **Hotel Andaluz** (downtown at 125 Second Street NW, 877-987-9090, www.hotelandaluz.com) is a Four Diamond property with a good restaurant and nice bar. Originally opened as the world's first Hilton Hotel, it has been extensively remodeled and is very attractive and comfortable.

The city's newest posh accommodations are found at **Hotel Chaco** (2000 Bellamah Avenue NW, 866-505-7829). Opened in 2017, the 118-room property is located right next to Old Town's museums, restaurants, and attractions, and includes an outdoor pool, beautiful gardens, and contemporary architecture.

Stepping down a notch in price is the **Best Western Rio Grande Inn** (just off I-140 at 1015 Rio Grande Boulevard NW, 800-959-4726, www.riograndeinn.com), with a year-round, heated outdoor pool and hot tub (great for unwinding those tired muscles!), large TVs, and minifridges in every room.

For a classy and relaxing bed-and-breakfast, check out **Adobe Garden at Los Ranchos** (641 Chavez Road NW, 505-345-1954, www.adobegarden.com). The two-story adobe structure is set among fields in the semirural Village of Los Ranchos in the North Valley and includes terrific breakfast, fireplaces, and other nice touches.

Nightlife

You can pick your poison from among hundreds of bars, music venues, cinema complexes, and other attractions for night owls in Albuquerque. For those who like to gamble, check out Sandia Resort and Casino (see Lodging), which also hosts nightly local and touring musical acts.

For a great "dive," complete with sticky floors, garish Polynesian decor, and live music, visit **Burt's Tiki Lounge** (515 Gold Avenue NW, 404-992-4376). Another downtown venue for live music and a young crowd is **Launchpad** (618 Central Avenue SE, 505-764-8887). If you care to do a little boot scootin', head to the state's largest country-and-western venue, **Dirty Bourbon Dance Hall and Saloon** (9800 Montgomery Boulevard NE, 505-296-2726), with its vast dance floor and two huge bars. Another classic country-and-western (and

Latin) outpost that's been swinging since 1979 in its current location, is the **Caravan East** (7605 Central Avenue NE, 505-265-7877). It has seen many a major country act grace its stage over the years and continues to book local and touring bands. Days and hours vary.

For a Prohibition-era cocktail served up in a swanky setting, check out the **Apothecary Lounge** (806 Central Avenue SE, 505-242-0040). Located on the roof of Hotel Parq Central, it provides panoramic views of sunsets, the Sandia Mountains, and the downtown skyline.

The city is also home to numerous craft breweries and taprooms, including **Marble** (111 Marble Avenue NW, 505-243-2739), **Tractor** (118 Tulane Drive SE and 1800 4th Street NW), **Bosque** (8900 San Mateo Boulevard NE, 505-750-7596), and **Nexus** (4730 Pan American Freeway East, just north of Montgomery, 505-242-4100); the latter two also serve food.

In Addition to Downhill Skiing

On the Mountain

Sandia Peak is in the process of building the state's first **Mountain Coaster**, a kind of partially enclosed sled or cart on steel rails that descends slopes via gravity, mimicking the experience of skiing or snowboarding downhill. The coaster will start near the top of the chairlifts and the tramway and run downhill for 2,825 feet between existing ski runs. It will become one of a handful of coasters found in Colorado and Utah and will operate year-round. It is expected to be functional in the summer of 2019. Pricing was not yet available at the time of this book's publication.

In Town

Albuquerque has lots of things to see and do besides skiing, and even in the dead of winter it is often snow-free, making it a great place to get out and tour its many attractions, historic sites, and events.

To understand the city's roots, and to peruse dozens of unique shops and restaurants, I always direct visitors first to **Old Town**. This is where the city got its start in

1706 by a handful of Hispanic farming families and where it was named after a Spanish duke—thus its nickname. Its plaza is charming, a quiet enclave in the bustling city, and facing it is an impressive Catholic church, San Felipe de Neri. If you are here at Christmas, be sure to do a walkabout to take in the plaza's display of luminarias—humble brown paper bags lit by candlelight. Indian artists sell handmade crafts under the portal on the east side of the plaza.

On the city's west edge is **Petroglyph National Monument**, one of the nation's greatest collections of prehistoric petroglyphs pecked into the basalt bounders and cliffs at the foot of seven small volcanoes. It is open daily (except Christmas). Another outdoor attraction is the **Rio Grande Nature Center**, which offers a glimpse into the ecology of the Rio Grande River, which bisects the city. In winter many waterfowl gather here, and there's great bird watching in general. A small museum provides displays and details on the region's natural history.

The **Albuquerque BioPark**, also in the valley near the river, includes a world-class zoo; extensive, beautifully landscaped botanical gardens (including lush greenhouses that are a delight on a winter's day); and a substantial aquarium focused on the aquatic life of the Rio Grande from source to sea.

Nearby is the **New Mexico Museum of Natural History and Science**, which includes a fantastic assembly of dinosaurs, a great planetarium, and IMAX theater.

"Duke City" is the world center of **hot-air ballooning**, and many commercial firms can take you up for an outing ranging from an hour to a half day. The city also has many excellent **running and biking paths**; particularly scenic are the trails in the **Elena Gallegos / Albert Simms Park** and **Bosque** areas (for details, see www.cabq.gov/parksandrecreation/recreation/bike). It is also home to many quality **golf courses**; with an average winter many are playable year-round.

Cultural attractions include the small but excellent **Albuquerque Museum of Art and History**—right across the street from the Museum of Natural History, the one-of-a-kind **National Hispanic Cultural Center**, and the highbrow **University of New Mexico Fine Arts Museum**. The All Indian Pueblo Council operates the **Indian Pueblo Culture Center** here, which offers a window into the realm of the region's Pueblo Indian people, including their rich artistic heritage, languages, foods (on-site restaurant serves traditional foods), and customs.

Sipapu

Address: Physical: 5224 NM 518, Vadito, NM 87579; Mail: Route Box 29, HC 65, Vadito, NM 87579

Ski Report: 800-587-2240

Information: 575-587-2240, 800-587-2240

Website: www.sipapunm.com

Facebook: Sipapu

Twitter: @SipapuNM

Instagram: @SipapuNM

Operating Hours: 9 a.m.–4 p.m. daily

Season: Generally Thanksgiving through Easter (with occasional later openings)

Mountain Profile

Base Elevation: 8,200 feet

Summit Elevation: hike-to 9,255 feet

Vertical Drop: 1,055 feet

Annual Snowfall: 190 inches

Area: 200 acres

Runs: 41 named

Longest Run: Smart Chicken to Sassafras to Bambi to Lower Bambi (two miles)

Lifts: Six (one quad, two triples, two magic carpets, and a platter)

Lift Capacity: 8,100 people per hour

Terrain Classification: Beginner: 20 percent; Intermediate: 40 percent; Advanced: 25 percent; Expert: 15 percent

Terrain Parks: Four

Snowmaking: About 70 percent of its runs

Seasonal Visits: Number not available

Backcountry Access Policy: Closed boundary

Season Highlights: The annual early February New Mexico Snow Bike Festival is the biggest event of its kind in the region, with free lessons, rentals, demos, and more. Later in February is the annual tribute to founder Lloyd Bolander.

Webcams: One, fixed

Amazing Facts: Sipapu was launched in 1952 by the Bolander family and is still family run. It is usually the first ski area in the state to open each winter.

The Bottom Line: Like the Little Engine That Could, tiny Sipapu ski resort should not be judged on size alone. Despite its modest vertical drop and acreage, the ski resort, with inexpensive on-site lodging, is very popular with families and has introduced thousands of people to the sport over its long history. It is the state's most affordable ski experience and is rarely crowded.

Getting Here

Driving

The ski area is located 25 miles southeast of Taos, 60 miles north of Santa Fe, and 61 miles northwest of Las Vegas, in the Carson National Forest. From Santa Fe, take US 84/285 north to Española, then NM 68 to NM 75. Proceed for about 20 miles east through Peñasco, Vadito, and Placitas to NM 518, and turn east (right) and continue for about 5 miles.

If coming from Taos, head south from town on NM 68, and in Ranchos de Taos turn left (east) onto NM 518 and proceed about 20 miles to the ski area.

If coming from Las Vegas, on I-25, take NM 518 northwest through Mora.

Flying

The closest major airport is the Albuquerque Sunport, and commercial flights also land in Santa Fe daily. The drive from Albuquerque takes about two and a half hours. You can rent a car in either Albuquerque (http://www.abqsunport.com/getting-around/rental-cars/) or Santa Fe (I suggest four-wheel drive; visit https://santafe.org/Visiting_Santa_Fe/About_Santa_Fe/Getting_Around_Santa_Fe/).

Train and Bus Links

Amtrak stops at Lamy, 20 minutes south of Santa Fe.

There is also a commuter rail service, the **Rail Runner** (www.nmrailrunner.com), which operates multiple times a day from Albuquerque to downtown Santa Fe. It includes a bus link in Albuquerque to the airport.

The North Central Rural Transportation District (i.e., the **Blue Bus**) has a seasonal bus running between Sipapu and Taos Mondays through Fridays. For more information and a schedule, call 866-206-0754 or visit www.RideTheBlueBus.com.

Services

Lift Tickets

Adult all-day all-lifts tickets run at least $44, half day at least $33; teens (13–20) full day at least $37, half day at least $28; juniors (7–12) full day at least $29, half day at least $22; seniors (61–69) full day at least $29, half day at least $22. Beginner tickets run just $19 or so. Free for children ages 6 and younger, fourth and fifth graders, 40-year-olds, 60-year-olds, and seniors over 70. Among many other discounts offered here are Car Load Day on 14 or so Wednesdays every season (six people for $50), Locals Appreciation Day on eight or so Thursdays (everyone qualifies, $25 for adult and teen tickets), and early-season and late-season rates. Half-day tickets begin at 1 p.m.

Rentals

The resort-based rental shop opens at 8 a.m. Its regular rental skis, boots, and poles run at least $16 for adults (ages 13 and up) and at least $13 for juniors; snowboards and boots run at least $28 for adults and $25 for juniors. The shop also carries a small selection of premier demo gear (at least $22 for skis, boots, and poles, and $35 for snowboards). Helmets run at least $8. They also rent snow blades (at least $16), snow bikes (at least $29), and snowshoes (at least $10). You can save time by filling out an online rental form.

Tuning
Available to the public on a walk-in basis. Located in the rental shop at the base.

Retail Shops
Olive's General Store provides guests with necessities ranging from gear to groceries, firewood to homemade fudge.

Ski School
Sipapu provides ski and snowboard lessons to anyone ages 3 and up at all ability levels. It offers up to three free lessons for first-timers (ages 7 and up) with purchase of full-day lift ticket. A two-hour group session for adults runs at least $60 (includes rentals) and at least $53 for teens. A one-hour private lesson runs at least $55. Family lessons are also available. With 24-hour advance reservations, one can also arrange telemark, ski bike, bike board, cross-country skiing, terrain park, and snowshoeing instruction. For reservations or details, call 800-587-2240 or e-mail skischool@SipapuNM.com.

Adaptive Ski Program
None

Childcare
None (ski school begins at age 3)

Mountain Tours
None

Lockers
Available in Sipapu's lodge and on the back patio

Cell Phone Service
There is a Wi-Fi hot spot in the Main Lodge, second floor. Decent coverage on the slopes and in most rooms.

First Aid
Located near the base lodge (575-587-2240)

Background

Sipapu (pronounced "SEE-pah-poo" and derived from a Pueblo Indian word designating the "place of emergence") was launched in 1952 by New Mexico native Lloyd Bolander and his wife, Olive, when they strung up a rope tow above the sparkling Rio Pueblo some 25 miles southeast of Taos, and began charging folks 50 cents for a day lift ticket. Aimed at families who could stay in their home lodge or adjoining cabins, the operation began with affordability in mind and maintains that approach to this day.

I have vague memories of spending a few

nights there at age 4 or 5. I recall huge masses of snow and dim gray light, the warmth of a wood-fired stove and stone fireplace, of getting wet and painfully cold but eager to get outdoors again, into the white world. I didn't ski, but we sledded and built snow forts and crawled around in the fluff. I recall the owners being wonderfully cordial, a lot of laughter among the adults, and a promise as we left that we would be back again the following year.

Over the years, with the support of Olive; his daughter, Sue; and his son, Bruce, the family added and replaced lifts, cut new trails, hand-built all of the resort's slopeside lodging, and opened a rental shop, restaurant, and store. Lloyd retired in 1984 but continued to run ski lessons and keep an eye on things for many more years. In 2004 he was inducted into the New Mexico Ski Hall of Fame. He passed away in 2014.

The resort's first quad chair was added for the 2015–2016 season, and its crew is always looking to add new features and improve its condition. They put a lot of emphasis on snowmaking, as it has the lowest base elevation in the state but remarkably is also usually the first area to open—sometimes in early November.

Harking back to its roots, one can find great deals here on combination lodging and lift tickets. But don't come expecting gourmet dining or nightlife. Here you make your own party. It's a totally no-frills experience, where many people will be skiing in Carharts or blue jeans. It is something of a throwback to a simpler era in skiing, when people didn't dress to impress or expect four-star amenities. It's simply about the joys of skidding on snow, of fresh air and exercise.

Mountain Highlights

Beginner Runs

The first-ever slopes are found just above the Main Lodge and are served by two surface lifts. But once stopping and basic turning have been mastered, beginners can ride the long triple (Chair 1) toward the summit and descend on **Sassafras** to **Bambi**.

They can also take Chair 1 and ski over to the poma (Lift 3) and take it a bit higher, coming down on **Brandy** or **Candy** to **Sassafras**. **Pinball**, off Sassafras, is a designated Kids Fun Zone.

Intermediate Runs

Most of the mountain is solid intermediate terrain; even some of the runs have been given a black diamond. Off Chair 3 is **Rufous** to **Thumper**, the wide **Butterfly** to **Rolling Rock**.

Way to skier's left is **Howdy**. A bit more demanding are **Uno** and **Lower Gamble**, running down the fall line under Chair 3. A good, newer option, running under the quad chair, is called **Fall Line**. One run, **Smart Chicken**, allows intermediates to access the resort's high point off Chair 4.

Advanced and Expert Runs

Sipapu splits its harder runs into "Most Difficult" and "Expert" classes. Most of these runs are found at the very summit, off Chair 4, but there's a handful that are accessible from Chair 3. **Upper Gamble**, a single black diamond, is right under Chair 3 and its moguls do provide a challenge. Running parallel to it is **No Whiners**. Off Chair 4 is **TS**, **No Caboose**, and **Worm**.

Good double blacks include **Oops** and **Indecision** off Chair 3, and **Wormwood** off Chair 4. Two of the most difficult runs, though short, are **Jip** and **Josh Chutes**.

Powder

Sipapu's "secret" is its fine powder skiing. With the acres of glades at the top of the mountain, one can uncover powder stashes here days after a storm, as most of the resort's clientele stick to the groomers or the terrain parks.

Specifically, the **Gamble Glades** and **Gamble Chutes** hold snow, as do the trees off Worm.

Bumps

Perhaps the best run here for bashing moguls is **Upper Gamble**. You can also seek out bumps at **Oops** and **Flower**.

Trees

A lot of thinning has been done on the upper mountain, creating acres of fine tree skiing when conditions allow. This includes significant sections of aspen tree skiing, rare in New Mexico, on runs like **No Caboose**, **Worm**, **Chopo's**, and the **Jip** and **Josh Chutes**.

Cruisers

Most of the resort's intermediate runs are groomed regularly and provide the best places to seek out terrain to let the skis run. Perhaps the best consistently is **Loose Caboose** to Thumper, and **Don Diego**.

Terrain Parks

Sipapu has four distinct terrain parks, including the only organic terrain parks in the state, **Playground** and **Flight School**, built entirely from resources found on the mountain. The advanced park, **Don Diego**, includes a 20-foot A-frame box with a dragon tongue (including two urban takeoffs and a straight mount), and a 38-foot tabletop gap jump. It often does not open until January or February. **Pedro's Park** is designed for beginner and intermediate riders.

Dining

The **Riverside Café**, on the second floor of the Main Lodge, is a full-service restaurant and bar serving New Mexican fare (try the red chile enchiladas or green chile stew), burgers, soups and sandwiches, plus breakfast meals. It operates 8 a.m.–8 p.m. daily. The Day Room is open to brown baggers.

Lodging

There's a small variety of accommodations, all owned by the ski area, just steps from the lift, including cabins, apartments, and the original Bolander home, **Adobe House**, which can sleep three to twelve people. Some accommodations include kitchenettes and wood-burning fireplaces, such as the magnificent stone fireplace in the large duplex. Dorm and bunkhouse rooms can run as little as $20. Some accommodations are even available for free under certain conditions (length of stay, time period, and a minimum number of lift tickets). There are also RV hookups and camping sites. For all rooms, check in at the Main Lodge (or after 4:30 p.m. at the night office several hundred yards down the road to the west). To make reservations, call 800-587-2240.

Many visitors stay in Taos or Santa Fe (see those chapters for options).

Nightlife

The lodge at the base has some open mic nights during holidays, but people basically entertain themselves here. Every Saturday 6 p.m.–9 p.m. is a free, open mic session in the Riverside Café. On Wednesdays at 6 p.m., free family movies are screened. Every Friday night visitors can enjoy a fish fry and classic ski film (cost is at least $9). For more options, visit Taos 25 miles away.

In Addition to Downhill Skiing

There is a small **game room** in the Main Lodge. **Tubing** and **sledding** are not allowed on the resort slopes but can be done safely nearby. Ask the lodge staff for details.

Snowshoeing can be enjoyed around the resort (but not on the slopes themselves) and on nearby national forest trails. Ask staff for details. There are also many options for **cross-country** skiing near Sipapu. See the "Taos Area" chapter in the cross-country section for details.

Ski Apache

Address: Physical: the west end of NM 532;
Mail: Box 220, Ruidoso, NM 88355

Ski Report: 575-464-1234

Information: 575-464-3600

Websites: Ski area: www.skiapache.com; town
of Ruidoso: www.visitruidoso.com or
www.ruidosonow.com; Mescalero Apache
Tribe: www.mescaleroapachetribe.com

Facebook: Ski Apache

Twitter: @skiapache

Instagram: @skiapache

Operating Hours: 9 a.m.–4 p.m.

Season: Generally Thanksgiving (with limited
terrain) through Easter

Mountain Profile

Base Elevation: 9,600 feet

Summit Elevation: hike-to 11,500 feet;
lift-served 11,400 feet

Vertical Drop: 1,900 feet

Annual Snowfall: 180 inches

Area: 750 acres

Runs: 55 named

Longest Run: Moonshine (1.24 miles)

Lifts: Ten (Apache Arrow eight-passenger
gondola, three quads, five triples, and a magic
carpet conveyor)

Lift Capacity: 17,380 skiers per hour

Terrain Classification: Beginner: 20 percent;
Intermediate: 60 percent; Expert: 20 percent

Terrain Parks: Two to three (depends on
conditions and time of visit)

Snowmaking: About 30 percent of the runs
serve beginner/intermediate skiers, including
one run from the summit.

Seasonal Visits: Number not available

Backcountry Access Policy: Closed boundary.

Season Highlights: A dummy gelände, a
torchlight parade, and fireworks kick off the
December holiday season. In early March join
in the Big Mountain Challenge to ski the most
vertical feet in a day (prizes include season
passes), and in mid-March enjoy the
pond-skimming and beach-body contests.
Throughout the season the resort hosts terrain
park competitions and Apache Star "fun"
races, open to all.

Webcams: At base, with six viewing angles

Amazing Facts: Ski Apache is one of only two
ski areas in the nation owned by an Indian
tribe, in this case the Mescalero Apaches. It
operates one of the world's longest zip lines.

The Bottom Line: The nation's southernmost
major ski area has surprisingly good conditions
because it sits on the flanks of the country's
southernmost 12,000-foot (and then some)
peak, Sierra Blanca. Its southern locale also
provides, arguably, the continent's mildest ski
area weather. Its eight-passenger gondola, the
only gondola in New Mexico, helps provide the
state's greatest lift capacity. With no
accommodations on-site, nearby Ruidoso
serves as its base of operations.

Getting Here

Driving

The ski area is located 18 miles northwest of
Ruidoso in southeastern New Mexico in the

Lincoln National Forest. It is about 200 miles southeast of Santa Fe, 180 miles southeast of Albuquerque, and 130 miles north of El Paso, Texas.

To get there coming from Albuquerque or Santa Fe, from Carrizozo (crossroads of US 380 and US 54) head east on US 380 for 8 miles, then turn right (south) onto NM 37, then right (west) onto NM 48 to Alto, and finally right (west) onto NM 532 (Ski Run Road) for 12 miles to the ski area. The last leg winds and climbs vigorously and requires four-wheel drive during a storm.

To get there from El Paso, take US 54 north to Alamogordo, then US 70 through Tularosa and on to Ruidoso. From midtown Ruidoso, head north 5 miles on NM 48 (Sudderth Drive), then turn left (west) onto NM 532 (Ski Run Road) for 12 miles to the ski area. The last leg winds and climbs vigorously and requires four-wheel drive during storms.

If coming from the west, from Las Cruces take US 70 east through Alamogordo and Tularosa and on to Ruidoso. Then follow directions above for El Paso drivers.

Flying

The closest major airport is in El Paso; Albuquerque is another option. Private planes can land at the Sierra Blanca Regional Airport (about 20 minutes from Ruidoso). You can rent a car in El Paso or Albuquerque (http://www.abqsunport.com/getting-around/rental-cars/).

Train and Bus Links

Amtrak stops in El Paso, 130 miles to the south.

Services

Lift Tickets

Ski Apache offers free lift tickets to beginners signing up to take a lesson.

Adults, full day at least $68, half day at least $49; teens (13–17), full day at least $59, half day at least $42; children (12 and younger), full day at least $48, half day at least $35; seniors (70 and older), full day at least $61, half day at least $44. Military adults at least $57, military child at least $43. Non-skiers can also buy a single-

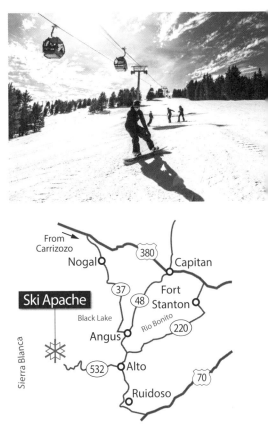

ride pass for the gondola—at least $17 for adults and $11 for children—providing access up to the Gazebo snack bar and warming area. Season passes and early-season discounts are available. Tickets can be bought online to avoid this morning task.

Rentals

The ski area has a large rental operation, carrying more than 1,500 pairs of skis and 300 snowboards. Located in the Main Lodge, it opens at 8 a.m. Its regular rental skis, boots, and poles run at least $24 for adults and $15 for juniors; snowboards run at least $32 for adults and $22 for juniors. The shop also carries a small selection of premier demo skis (at least $37 for skis alone; helmet rentals $7). For details, call 575-464-3661.

The town of Ruidoso also has many rental shops. Among them are the following:

A-Frame Ski Shop (1016 Mechem Drive, 575-258-5656), which also has a batch of small cabins for rent.

St. Bernard (420 Mechem Drive, 575-257-7777) is a huge facility with lots of options on renting or buying ski or snowboarding gear and apparel. Open 8 a.m.–6 p.m. and later on holidays.

Ski Ruidoso (1133 Mechem Drive, 575-258-3024) opens at 7 a.m. and stays open late on Fridays.

Alto Ski Shop (874 NM 48, in Alto at Ski Run Road, 575-336-4386) is great for convenience.

Tuning

The ski area's rental shop in the Main Lodge can provide tune-ups and other repair work.

Retail Shops

Summit Sports in the base complex carries all basic ski apparel and accessories, plus logo merchandise.

Ski School

Ski Apache introduces *lots* of people to skiing and employs around 70 certified instructors. A two-hour adult group session runs at least $91; for kids at least $83. A group adult snowboard lesson is at least $100; a kids' lesson is at least $89. Prices include lift ticket and rentals. A one-hour private lesson for any and all ability levels runs at least $85 for adults and $65 for children.

There is also a program called **Adventure Center** for children ages 4–11, including all-day or half-day ski instruction, lunch, and lift ticket. For details, call 575-464-3643. Children younger than 6 years old receive free lift tickets.

In addition, there are special package deals for first-ever skiers. This includes five lessons and five lift ticket deals; if you complete the lessons, you qualify for a free pass for the remainder of the season.

Adaptive Ski Program

A local nonprofit provides equipment and instruction in alpine skiing, Nordic skiing, and snowboarding for people of all ages with a variety of disabilities. Call 575-464-3193 or visit www.skiapacheadaptivesports.com for details.

Childcare

Full day costs at least $140 (includes lunch) or $150 (includes lunch and equipment). Reservations suggested: 575-464-3643.

Mountain Tours

None

Lockers

There are numerous small lockers found in the base lodge.

Cell Phone Service

Coverage across the mountain

First Aid

There are Ski Patrol centers at the top of the gondola and at the bottom of the gondola in the base area. Call 575-464-3621 for details.

Background

This ski area, which seems an impossibility amid the Chihuahua Desert of south-central New Mexico, was launched in 1961 as Sierra Blanca Ski Resort by oil magnet Robert O. Anderson and general manager Kingsbury Pitcher, who would go on to acquire Ski Santa Fe a few years later.

High altitude is what makes skiing possible here. The area is located in the Sacramento Mountains beneath the summit of the nation's southernmost mountain higher than 12,000 feet, Sierra Blanca (White Mountain) Peak, located just outside the resort's boundary.

In 1962 the state's first, and only, gondola was added to the area's original three pomas, attracting a phenomenal 25,000 skiers in its second year of operations. In 1963, the

Mescalero Apache Tribe, whose original home-lands encompassed the region, bought out the business, becoming the nation's first tribe to own a ski area. It remains just one of two such operations nationwide—the other being Sunrise in Arizona. The tribe brought in Roy Parker as general manager, a position he retained for more than 30 years. In 1984 the area's name was changed to Ski Apache.

The distinctive, modernist-style Main Lodge was designed by the award-winning architect Victor Lundy, with its soaring wooden columns echoing the surrounding tall pines.

In a wet winter you can stand on top of five feet or more of snow and look west down some 7,000 feet to sparkling White Sands National Monument, where horny toads dart about yucca and cactus, their eyes glinting in the relentless sun. The greatest vertical displacement in the state offers magnificent views southward to mountain ranges marching toward Mexico and eastward onto the Great Plains.

In the summer of 2012, a massive fire roared through the ski area, destroying its original gondola and two other chairs (all since replaced) and killing large tracts of pines. The ski area is slowly clearing the dead and downed wood, which will eventually open up significant new skiing terrain.

This winter and summer playground is populated predominately with West Texans fleeing their level lands and heat. Thus, the area has a preponderance of beginner and intermediate terrain but also surprisingly abundant terrain for expert skiers, and it even offers some tree skiing when conditions allow.

With no development in the base area other than a basic lodge, all visitors stay, dine, and pursue other activities in the town of Ruidoso, which has a huge number of lodging options, restaurants, small shops, and other amenities.

Mountain Highlights

Beginner Runs

Ski Apache has introduced tens of thousands of beginners to the sport and has ample runs for first-timers and those learning the basics. A triple chair at the base provides access to a broad, gentle learning area, **Bunny Slope**, and another base quad steps it up a bit, letting beginners maneuver down **Easy Street**. More adventuresome beginners can then head up Chair 7 to tackle **Lower Moonshine** and **Lower Spruce**.

While the area does not have a true beginner run descending from the summit, beginners can get close to the top by riding the Lincoln Chair, descending on **Sierra Blanca**, which winds its way back and forth across the mountain.

Intermediate Runs

Many intermediate skiers happily spend entire days doing laps on **Capitan**, the consistently pitched and always immaculately groomed run right above the Main Lodge. With its own short triple chair, it's a great place to kick up your technique a notch.

Apache Bowl, in the cupped valley beneath towering Sierra Blanca Peak, holds some great intermediate terrain. After admiring the stunning scenery from the top, make long turns down the open bowl and into the funnels and natural half-pipes that drain from its bottom. These pipes, in a good snow year, are a delight for snowboarders and intrepid skiers. If you descend too far you will have to ski all the way to the bottom, but the bowl is served by its own triple chair, making this a popular part of the mountain.

The **Elk Lift subarea** is also great terrain for strong intermediates. Even though most of its runs are designated as expert slopes, they are groomed regularly and are not too steep.

More good runs for intermediates are found off the gondola and Chair 1, on the far west side of the area. **East of Eden**, **Meadows**, **Chino**, and **Ambush** all converge on **Moonshine Gulch**, leading you back to the lifts.

Expert Runs

The area's toughest runs are the handful of slopes running parallel to one another under and near Chair 1, runs like **Screaming Eagle**, **Dead End**, **Terrible**, **Incredible**, and **Mescalero**. Probably my favorite is the run under the Lincoln Chair, which is triple the length of the previously noted expert runs. Right next to it is the similarly long and nicely pitched gondola lift line.

Powder

With most of the resort's clientele consisting of novices, powder stashes lay untouched here for days and offer up opportunities for some notable powder skiing. Dip into the spacious woods below **Game Trail** pocketed with small openings, which eventually spits you out onto a well-traveled gully, Upper Deep Freeze— beware of the major drops onto it at certain points. You can also poke into the trees that separate Mescalero, Terrible, Incredible, Dead End, Screaming Eagle, and Rover, though fires and insect kills in recent years have fouled much of these forests.

In good snow years, the wide-open space of **Apache Bowl** and **South Face** offer almost-endless possibilities for powder skiing.

Bumps

Ski Apache used to be known for its tough bump runs, but most are now tamed by regular grooming. However, a few still are allowed to bump up, such as skier's left on **Capitan**. Laps here will wear out even the fittest skier.

Trees

Ski Apache used to have surprisingly good tree skiing, and there are still pockets where you can slip past the screening pines facing the runs and into the woods, finding narrow lanes and small glades. This is still the case in the large swatch of forest below Game Trail. You can spend lots of time exploring the many lines in here, which deposit onto Upper Deep Freeze. Be careful of the high banks above Deep Freeze at the bottom of these woods— you have to carefully pick spots to ease over this transition.

But much of the other tree skiing terrain, the island woods between Mescalero and Rover, have been devastated by fire and insect invasions, and fallen trees now block much of this terrain. The resort hopes to clear these woods in the future.

Cruisers

With the careful grooming done here, and generally modest pitch found on most terrain, Ski Apache is a great place to let the skis run and carve those train-track turns. Game Trail is a long, leisurely descent along the east boundary, and links up to **Elk Ridge** and Capitan for a top-to-bottom screamer. **Chino** to **Moonshine Gulch** offers up another extended cruise.

Terrain Parks

There are usually two to three modest terrain parks operating here, depending on conditions: a beginner park called **Easy Street**, an intermediate area called **Moonshine**, and the advanced area, **Competition Park**, with jumps, tubes, and rails.

Dining

On the Mountain

The primary place to eat at the ski area, the **Eagle Café**, is located in the Main Lodge. The cafeteria, with indoor and deck seating, has a daily special or two and soups during peak periods, along with burgers, burritos, wings, sandwiches, and such. Also in the Main Lodge, operating at peak times, is the **Daily Grind**, specializing in coffee, pastries, ready-made sandwiches, and other light fare. Yet another option in the Main Lodge during busy periods is **Arrowhead Grill**, serving tacos, burritos (with choice of beef, pork, or chicken), salads, and snacks. In the gondola station area is the **Plaza Grill**, an outdoor venue, with a simple menu and panoramic view of the mountain.

The Main Lodge is also home to the **Spirit Bar**, with nice views of the mountain from inside and from its outdoor deck. The **Elk Chair Lodge** in the subarea of the same name also has a lodge with basic food services and a spacious patio for sun seekers.

On the mountain, at the gondola summit, is the **Gazebo**, a yurt structure open weekends and holidays. It carries premade sandwiches, candy bars, soft drinks, bottled water, and other grab-and-go items. Another occasional food outlet with a limited menu is the small **Moonshine Burger Stand**, at the base of Chair 1, top of Chair 7. The **Lookout Snack Bar** is found at the top of the Apache Bowl Chair.

In Town

Ruidoso is packed with places to eat. One of the best has to be **Michael J's** (601 Mechem Drive, 575-257-9559, www.michaeljsrestaurant.com), which specializes in Italian food. This ranges from a great Caesar or caprese salad and delicious minestrone soup to house-made ravioli, chicken piccata, and solid steak or salmon entrées. The team spirit here gives it a friendly vibe, with excellent service. Beer and good wine choices add up to a nice meal.

Southern New Mexico is cattle country, so a visit to **Rancher's Steak and Seafood** (2823 Sudderth Drive, 575-257-7540, www.facebook.com/RanchersRuidoso) is appropriate for excellent cuts of meat plus delicious alternatives to the red meat diet. It also has a full bar.

Cornerstone Bakery Café (359 Sudderth Drive, 575-257-1842, www.cornerstonebakerycafe.com) has good coffee and serves up a nice selection of egg dishes and house-made pastries.

Farley's (1200 Mechem Drive, 575-258-5676, www.farleyspub.com) has stood the test of time, having commenced business in 1995. With pub grub and a full bar, and one of the first places to eat and drink when coming into Ruidoso from Ski Apache, it's a popular gathering spot in town après-ski.

There are a number of good places for New Mexican fare. **Tina's Café** (522 Sudderth Drive, 575-257-8930, www.facebook.com/tinascaferuidoso) has an excellent chicken tamale and pork puff pastries, plus a nice fireplace and seating next to the Ruidoso Rover. **Casa Blanca** (501 Mechem Drive, 575-257-2495, www.facebook.com/CasaBlancaRuidoso) has been dishing up good New Mexican food for decades. **Chef Lupe's** (1101 Sudderth Drive, 575-257-4687, www.facebook.com/pages/Chef Lupes/344714332246630) is a newish entry into this field. Also suggested is **Porky's** (2306 Sudderth Drive, 575-257-0544), a tiny eatery with tasty breakfast burritos; also open for lunch.

And there are even a few spots for vegetarians, including the pizza-centric **Treehouse Café** (118 West Shore Drive in Alto,

575-336-8444, www.facebook.com/treehouse-cafealto) and **Grill Caliente** (2800 Sudderth Drive, 575-630-0224, www.grillcaliente.com).

Lodging

There are no overnight accommodations at the ski area. The closest motels are found in Alto at the bottom of the access road, with many sleeping choices—from tiny cabins and motels to spacious homes, condominiums, and hotels. There are also numerous RV parks.

The **Inn of the Mountain Gods** (287 Carrizo Canyon Road, five miles southwest of town, 888-262-0478, www.innofthemountaingods.com) tops the list. Also owned by the Mescalero Apache Tribe, the AAA four-diamond property is a true resort, featuring a large casino with all the Las Vegas–style games, a large lake for fishing, a wonderful 18-hole golf course, an indoor swimming pool, a sauna, a steam room, a 15-person hot tub, a game arcade, year-round sporting clay range, and shops. It also includes a 2,000-seat performance hall. There's a sports bar in the casino and the very attractive **Wendell's Lounge**. Restaurants include the upscale **Wendell's Steak and Seafood**, as well as casual options. A gift shop serves up coffee to go and breakfast bites. The inn also runs a shuttle to the ski area (at least $20 per person).

The three-story lobby windows provide beautiful views of the lake and of Sierra Blanca wrapped in storm clouds or shining in the sun. The inn takes its decorative theme from cultural motifs of the tribe, making this a one-of-a-kind facility. Under the wise leadership of former chairman Wendell Chino, the tribe bought Ski Apache in 1963 and simultaneously went about opening the country's first deluxe resort owned by an Indian tribe. The best views at the 273-room hotel face the lake and Sierra Blanca on the fifth and sixth floors.

Comfort Inn (2709 Sudderth Drive, 866-859-5146 or 575-257-2770) is a good chain option. Much of the lodging along the main thoroughfares of Mechem and Sudderth is marred by traffic noise, but this place is quieter and includes indoor and outdoor pools and hot tubs; LCD TVs with HBO, refrigerators, microwaves, irons, ironing boards hair

dryers, coffee makers, clock radios, and free high-speed wired and wireless Internet in each room; a business center; fitness center; guest laundry; and free hot breakfast.

Shadow Mountain Lodge and Cabins (107 Main Road, 575-257-4886, www.smlruidoso.com) is a popular choice, with both private cabins and single rooms, some with fireplaces, kitchenettes, and Jacuzzi tubs. It boasts pretty grounds, a hot tub, a barbecue setup, and other amenities—plus it's quiet.

Condohotel (1103 Mechem Drive, 800-545-9017, 575-258-5200, www.ruidosoreservations.com) can provide a wide range of accommodations ranging from one to eight bedrooms, including attractive homes, condominiums, and cabins (some with hot tubs and fireplaces), scattered around town.

The **Lodge at Sierra Blanca** (107 Sierra Blanca Drive, 575-258-5500, 866-211-7727, www.thelodgeatsierrablanca.com) is off the main roads, facing the golf course, and is a bit more upscale than many town accommodations. It has a pool, a hot tub, Wi-Fi, and breakfast.

The **Escape Resort at Ruidoso** (1016 Mechem Road, 888-762-8551, 575-258-1234, www.theescaperesort.com) is one of the nicest—and priciest—properties in the region, with refined decor, spacious casitas, full kitchens, steam baths, and gas fireplaces, all set on five forested acres.

Sitzmark Chalet Inn (627 Sudderth Drive, 575-257-4140, 800-658-9694, www.sitzmark-chalet.com) is on the highway but is a charming, spotlessly clean, affordable old-school property, with rooms for one to four people, some with fireplaces.

2 Ruidoso Redheads (www.facebook.com/2ruidosoredheads) is a business specializing in visitor services of all kinds, from finding lodging and arranging dining, transportation, and activities. Let them figure it all out for you!

Nightlife

The **Spirit Bar** in the Main Lodge at the ski area can rock après-ski but turns off its lights at 6 p.m., and the party moves off the mountain and into Ruidoso.

There are a handful of fun places in town to throw back a few, shoot pool, perhaps do some dancing. A drinking and dancing institution is midtown's **Win Place or Show** (2516 Sudderth Drive, 575-257-9982, www.facebook.com/pages/Win-Place-and-Show/109483032423294), also simply known as WPS, which has presented live music every night since 1952! Its gleaming hardwood floor is *the* place to boot scoot in "Row-dosa." Toby Keith has been known to drop in and sing a song.

Right across the street is classic blues bar meets the Wild West at **Quarters Saloon and Grill** (2535 Sudderth Drive, 575-257-9535, www.facebook.com/QuartersNightclub). It's been in business for decades and occasionally features live music, as well as pool, darts, and foosball. Not recommended as a place to eat if it's crowded.

Rio Grande Grill and Tap Room (441 Mechem Drive, 575-808-8456, www.sierrablancabrewery.com) is a great place to drop in and get to know some fellow beer drinkers. It's a friendly spot with some excellent New Mexican brews to be sampled and a great choice to grab lunch or dinner. In fact, it's one of the better kitchens in town, with appetizers, soups and salads, sandwiches and burgers, pasta dishes, grilled entrées, and homemade desserts.

There's also the large and newish **Grace O'Malley's Irish Pub** (2331 Sudderth Drive, 575-630-0219, www.graceomalleys.com), which has live music many weekend nights, plus darts and pool, along with 24 beers on tap and a full restaurant.

The **Inn of the Mountain Gods** (287 Carrizo Canyon Road, five miles southwest of town, 888-262-0478, www.innofthemountaingods.com) also presents major touring bands, comedians, and other entertainment almost every weekend year-round in its spacious Events Center.

Also see entry for the **Spencer Theater** below.

In Addition to Downhill Skiing

On the Mountain

The ski area's **Windrider Ziptour** is one of the longest zip lines in the world. Split into three legs, it runs almost 9,000 linear feet from its

start elevation of 11,489 feet. It operates year-round (weather permitting) and has parallel cables allowing two riders to descend at once. Split into three legs, the entire experience takes about one and a half hours to complete. Reservations are suggested (575-464-3633).

Limited gambling, in the form of slot machines, is also found at the ski area. They are located on the second floor of the Elk Lodge.

Sledding at the ski area is not allowed.

In Town

Ruidoso, a major tourist center in summer, has a wide variety of things to do and see even in winter, when attractions like go-cart tracks are shut down.

The **Ruidoso Winter Park** snow-play area (north edge of town at the bottom of Ski Run Road off NM 48, 575-336-7079, www.ruidoso winterpark.com) is a wonderful, safe place to go tubing, with giant tubes holding up to six adults. Some courses include twists, bumps, jumps, and bobsled-like curves. A snowmaking system ensures good conditions most of the winter, and there's a special area for the very young. Multiple magic carpet lifts transport you uphill, with rentals on-site (including clothing), a snack bar with excellent pizza, and free marshmallow roasting at the campfire. It is open until 8 or 9 p.m. on select nights.

The **Hubbard Museum of the American West** (26301 US 70, in Ruidoso Downs, 575-378-4142, www.hubbardmueum.org), an affiliate of the Smithsonian Institute, provides exhibitions and insights covering the Indian, Hispanic, and American settler history of the region through its more than 10,000-piece collection. Open daily.

Another notable attraction is the **Spencer Theater** (about ten miles northeast of town on Airport Highway / NM 220, 575-336-4800, www.spencertheater.com). Said to be rated among the ten best acoustic venues in the world, the 554-seat performance venue has a

seven-story flyspace overhead for storing sets, an architectural form that mimics the nearby mountain range, and an amazing glass reception space graced with several glass sculptures by Dale Chihuly. If you can catch a show here, go! It also offers public tours. Call for times.

Ruidoso is also a regional center for sale of arts and crafts, with dozens of **galleries** and numerous one-of-a-kind **gift shops**.

Nearby

You can find a slew of cool places to visit and things to do in the surrounding region, especially if you have an interest in western history and culture or the area's scenic and ecological riches. **Lincoln**, New Mexico (about an hour away) was the center for the 1877–1881 conflict that brought Billy the Kid to the world's attention. You can visit the jail he once escaped from (and see the bullet hole he put in a stairway wall), drop by a fine, small state museum—which also documents the fascinating story of the Buffalo Soldiers who were once stationed at nearby **Fort Stanton** (today a state monument)—or check out other historic sites, then enjoy a lunch at the storied Dolan House.

Also about an hour away, in **Capitan**, is a museum and nature center that documents the life of Smokey Bear, who was found nearby in the 1920s after a forest fire. And also about an hour away, in **Carrizozo**, is the state's largest photo venue, the Tularosa Gallery of Photography, as well as several other galleries, some down-home places to eat, and other artsy attractions. Just outside Carrizozo is **Valley of Fire State Park**, which presents views of snow-capped Sierra Blanca Peak rising over the sun-cooked black lava flows of this ecopark, and the ghost town of **White Oaks**. And about 70 miles from Ruidoso is **White Sands National Monument**, one of America's more sublime and alluring landscapes.

Ski Santa Fe

Address: Physical: at end of NM 475; Mail: PO Box 2108, Santa Fe, NM 87504

Ski Report: Online only

Information: 505-982-4429

Websites: www.skisantafe.com, www.santafe.org, and www.santafe.com

Facebook: skisantafe

Twitter: @skisantafe

Instagram: @skibueno

Operating Hours: 9 a.m.–4 p.m. daily; late season, 9:30 a.m.–4:30 p.m.

Season: Generally Thanksgiving through first Sunday of April

Mountain Profile

Base Elevation: 10,350 feet

Summit Elevation: lift-served 12,075 feet

Vertical Drop: 1,725 feet

Annual Snowfall: 225 inches

Area: 660 acres

Runs: 82 named

Longest Run: Fall-line run: Gay Way (4,600 feet); Catwalk: Sunset (4,900 feet)

Lifts: Seven (one quad, two triples, two doubles, two surface)

Lift Capacity: 9,350 skiers per hour

Terrain Classification: Beginner: 20 percent; Intermediate: 40 percent; Expert: 40 percent

Terrain Parks: One

Snowmaking: About 50 percent of the runs, including all beginner and most intermediate terrain

Seasonal Visits: 150,000 skiers per year

Backcountry Access Policy: An open-boundary policy prevails here, but there are extreme avalanche hazards in some directions and several skiers have been lost.

Season Highlights: In mid-March, it usually hosts the annual Tess Horan Ascension, an uphill/downhill race. Late March brings on the Gladfelter Memorial Bump Run, with some nifty prizes in many divisions to the best on skis and boards. Throughout January and February, enjoy live music on the deck at Totemoff's, along with a sampling of local suds.

Webcams: Several locations, with viewer control

Amazing Facts: North America's fifth-highest base elevation, 10,350 feet

The Bottom Line: Ski Santa Fe is a remarkably good midsized ski area, with a terrific variety of terrain, dependable snow, and tremendous views. It is one of only two state ski areas that allow free "uphill skiing." The charming, world-class arts, culture, and dining town of Santa Fe is just 30 minutes from the slopes.

Getting Here

Driving

The ski area is located 16 miles from Santa Fe at the very end of NM 475. Curvy with some steep pitches, the road climbs more than 3,000 vertical feet and can be impassable in two-wheel-drive cars during storms. From the corner of Paseo de Peralta and Washington Street, head north two blocks to Artist Road and turn right (east). The road winds up through Hyde State Park and onto the ski area.

Flying

The closest major airport is the Albuquerque Sunport, and commercial flights also land in

Santa Fe daily. The drive from Albuquerque to Santa Fe town is one hour. You can rent a car in either Albuquerque (http://www.abqsunport.com/getting-around/rental-cars/) or Santa Fe (I suggest four-wheel-drive; visit https://santafe.org/Visiting_Santa_Fe/About_Santa_Fe/Getting_Around_Santa_Fe/). You can also take a paid shuttle (see below).

Train and Bus Links

Amtrak stops at Lamy, 20 minutes south of Santa Fe.

There is also a commuter rail service, the **Rail Runner** (www.nmrailrunner.com), which operates multiple times a day from Albuquerque to downtown Santa Fe. It includes a bus link in Albuquerque to the airport.

In 2015, public transportation, the **Blue Bus**, from the city of Santa Fe to the ski area was launched. One-way fare is $5 (exact change required), with drop-off at the main entrance. There are multiple pickup and drop-off points in town, including the Santa Fe Depot to access the Rail Runner. For more information and a schedule, call 866-206-0754 or visit www.RideTheBlueBus.com.

Shuttles

Twin Hearts Express: 800-654-9456, 575-751-1201. Daily service heading north from Albuquerque Sunport at 11:30 a.m., 1:30 p.m.,

3:30 p.m., and 5:30 p.m. to the Santa Fe Airport. It departs the Santa Fe Airport for Albuquerque daily at 8:30 a.m., 10:30 a.m., 12:30 p.m., and 3 p.m. The fee is about $30 one way, $55 round trip.

Services

Lift Tickets

Adult all-day, all-lifts tickets run at least $75, students (13–23) at least $60, kids at least $52, and seniors at least $56. Beginner tickets run at least $38. Half-day adult tickets are at least $60, and run from start of day to 12:30 p.m., and 12:30 p.m. to end of day (start and end 30 minutes later in late season). Kids under 46 inches in height ski free, as do Super Seniors (ages 72 and up). There are discounts, including multiple-day tickets and for active-duty military. The 6 Pack Card is a transferable pass providing for six days of skiing or boarding. The Peak Plus Card saves $25 on all mountain lift tickets at Ski Santa Fe or Sandia Peak. There are also group discounts. For details, e-mail info@skisantafe.com.

Rentals

The resort's new rental shop really improved this facet of its operations. It opens at 8 a.m. The shop's regular rental skis, boots, and poles run at least $32 for adults and $24 for juniors 12 years and younger; snowboards run at least $38 for adults and $30 for juniors. The shop also carries a selection of high-performance snowboards and skis (at least $36 for skis alone, at least $34 for boards). Helmets run $12.

As noted, there are options in town, and on the access road. Here are some choices:

Cottam's (740 Hyde Park Road, 505-982-0942, cottamsskishops.com), located in Hyde State Park right on the ski area access road, rents skis, boards, cross-country skis, snowshoes, and snow blades. They offer an online registration and reservation system.

Alpine Sports (121 Sandoval Street, 505-983-5155, www.alpinesportsonline.com) is Santa Fe's oldest ski shop. Launched in 1963, it provides excellent customer service, a wide range of rentals—including high-end demos—sales of clothing and accessories, and excellent tuning work.

Ski Tech (905 South St. Francis Drive,

505-983-5512, www.skitechsantafe.com) rents skis, boards, boots, and poles, as well as snowshoes, snow pants, bibs, and helmets. It offers the city's only rental delivery service. Economy ski packages begin at $29 a day; premium demos at least $45. They also do tune-ups.

Tuning

Anything from a complete tune-up to a quick edge job or waxing can be done here. Located in the rental shop at the base.

Retail Shops

The Ski Santa Fe Sports Shop in the base building, La Casa Lodge, sells a wide variety of clothing and accessories, plus Ski Santa Fe logo merchandise.

Ski School

Ski Santa Fe provides ski and snowboard lessons to anyone over age 10, at all ability levels. A two-hour group session runs at least $56, and two group sessions run at least $76. A one-hour private lesson runs at least $105.

Adaptive Ski Program

Ski Santa Fe, and its sister area, Sandia Peak, offer adaptive ski programs such as ski lessons for adults and children (5 years and older) with a wide array of physical and mental disabilities. Instruction is available in two track, three track, four track, blind, deaf, mono-ski, bi-ski, and snowboarding. They work with people suffering from developmental delays, spinal cord injury, cerebral palsy, amputation, spina bifida, traumatic brain injury, muscular dystrophy, Down syndrome, multiple sclerosis, critical vision or hearing challenges, attention deficit / learning issues, autism spectrum disorder, polio, and stroke. For details or reservations, call 505-995-9858.

Childcare

Chipmunk Corner is kid central at Ski Santa Fe. My own two children attended it while daddy skied, and they had a fun introduction on and in the snow. Nursery and daycare services are offered for children ages 3 months–3 years. Potty-trained children are set up in the Snow Play program, with outdoor and indoor play and lunch with a movie. Their ski slope, isolated from any other skiers, includes a magic carpet surface lift. Full day costs at least $110. A

day of rentals, instruction, and lift tickets, plus supervision, for youth ages 3–11 costs at least $145. Reservations required: 505-988-9636.

Mountain Tours

None

Lockers

Found on the ground floor of La Casa Lodge

Cell Phone Service

Very spotty coverage overall; none in the base area, okay at summit

First Aid

The primary care center (505-992-5086) is located below the outdoor deck of La Casa Lodge, the base building, facing the ski slopes. Ski patrol also has a nifty cabin at the top of the Tesuque Peak chair. In town, there are a number of businesses providing urgent care.

Background

Today's Ski Santa Fe, in name and location, is the newest incarnation of the dream of an early band of ski pioneers in the American Southwest to bring the sport to New Mexico.

In 1935 Ferdinand Koch and Daniel Kelly, president and vice president, respectively, of the Santa Fe Chamber of Commerce, made a presentation to their members about their recent trip to New England, where they had been introduced to new sport of skiing. Could skiing be the key in New Mexico, they asked, to making tourism a year-round economic force in Santa Fe? Koch brought in an expert on the topic, Graeme McGowan of Denver, who had recently helped launch Berthoud Pass in Colorado. McGowan arrived in February 1936 and made a survey of possible skiing terrain above town. He produced a remarkable leather-bound prospectus—complete with a fascinating hand-drawn map and black-and-white photos—for the newly formed Santa Fe Winter Sports Club, whose members included Koch, Kelly, T. B. Catron, Hunter Clarkson, and other community leaders.

The document produced a flurry of activity, and on January 21, 1937, skiing commenced on a 750-foot rope tow at Hyde State Park, which then lay at the end of the mountain road. Bus service was provided along with a temporary food concession, drawing an enthusiastic response. That summer, the stone lodge that still graces the park was built by the Civilian Conservation Corps.

In 1947 the road was extended to Big Tesuque Creek, and two rope tows—one an impressive 2,000 feet long—were installed, with engines donated by Koch, Clarkson, Charles LeFeber, and Clarence Via. Overseeing their operation was Buzz Bainbridge, who also worked at what is now Sandia Peak. He recalls putting a lit blowtorch to the Cadillac engine block at Hyde Park to get it warmed up, then driving four miles up the road to Big Tesuque, where he would start the lift there, then come back down to Hyde Park to fire up the Caddy.

By September 1948, the road was pushed still higher, to its present terminus, with the support of Eleanor Roosevelt. In March 1949, Koch formed an investment company, Sierras de Santa Fe, to finance construction of a chairlift at the new site. In 1950, Swiss German Ernie Blake, who would go on to fame as the founder of Taos Ski Valley, was brought aboard as manager, the job that brought him to the region. A used cable from the Eureka Mine in Silverton, Colorado, was secured, and another made in Sheffield, England, in 1888. With seats pulled from old B-24 bombers and a diesel engine donated by Koch, the state's first chairlift was cobbled together. It rose a glorious 630 vertical feet, up today's Thunderbird run. In 1954, Koch helped negotiate the sale of the Forest Service lease to Joe Juhan of Texas, who would eventually turn over its operation to Kingsbury Pitcher.

Kingsbury was a superb skier, the first American to be hired in the elite Sun Valley Ski School and also worked in the earliest days of Aspen with Friedl Pfeifer. The Pitchers of Santa Fe made major investments, including first a giant poma to a point just below Tesuque Peak, followed eventually by a triple chair, which topped out at a lung-searing 12,053 feet, making it for many years the continent's highest lift-served skiing. Also putting in some years here was the ubiquitous Pete Totemoff, jack-of-all-trades and one hell of a ski racer, who also played founding roles at Sandia Peak and Taos. Ski Santa Fe's mid-mountain dining area and bar is named after him.

In October 1984, the Abruzzo family of Albuquerque bought the area. Ben Abruzzo

had helped build Sandia Peak ski area and its impressive aerial tram. His heirs—particularly Benny Abruzzo and his grandson, Ben Jr.—continue to run Ski Santa Fe. Among many improvements they've completed was the addition of the Millennium chair, in 2006–2007, which tops out at 12,075 feet.

With the fifth-highest base of all North American ski areas, and one of the highest summits—in a region known for its startlingly clear skies and powerful sunlight—a day here is often magical. The air is different, the light changed. While town might be bathed in a golden glow, just 30 minutes away and up, you could be in a raging storm, or conversely, above the fog that sits at the foot of the Sangre de Cristo Mountains, where the Rocky Mountains begin and end. The views are often 200 miles or more of Earth: 100 miles north to the San Juans of Colorado, 100-plus miles to Sierra Blanca Peak down south by Ruidoso and west to Mount Taylor near the Arizona line.

Peaks topping the tree line, including nearby Santa Fe Baldy at 12,600 feet, rise above you, with radical chutes dropping into the Nambé Valley below snaggy Lake Peak. In a good winter the trees across the top of the mountain will be covered with rime and snow, mute sentinels to winter's onslaught. I've been here on 10-degree days with 30 miles-per-hour wind, and the last 200 yards of the upper chairs can be brutal. It's a primordial environment locked in deep winter, home to snowshoe hares and foxes.

Meanwhile, down in town, different kinds

of animals roam—the hip, urban kind. Santa Fe has one of the nation's best food scenes, world-class museums, hundreds of art galleries, one-of-a kind shops of all stripes, nightclubs, installation art centers, and more. It's a great combo, and a big part of why many people live here.

Mountain Highlights

Beginner Runs

The easiest terrain is found right at the bottom of the ski area, served by the Pine Flats beginner conveyor, a sedate chair, and the run **Easy Street**. Largely cut off from the rest of the ski area, it's a tranquil zone dedicated to beginners and has its own slow chairlift and a surface conveyor lift.

But more competent beginners can soon be skiing off the top of the quad chair, accessing runs like **Santa Fe Trail** (the easiest way down from the quad), or **Davey Lane** to **Midland** to **Third Way** to **Lower Broadway**. **Lower Broadway**, under the quad chair, runs straight down the fall line at a low angle, making it great beginner terrain.

Intermediate Runs

There are a lot of choices for intermediates here, especially off the quad. An obvious choice is **Upper Broadway**, under the chair. It is always nicely groomed and has a nice sustained pitch. **Thunderbird** is a run many people overlook. One of the area's oldest runs, being its first chair line, it often hides some powder on the edges of its challenging mogul fields. Get to it via Crossover if its top pitch looks too steep. The most prominent choice on the bottom of the mountain is **Open Slope**, another of the early runs here when the area was largely devoid of trees following a fire in the late 1800s. It is broad and always nicely groomed.

Signs of the fire are still evident higher on the mountain off the Tesuque Peak chair. At the top of **Gay Way** you'll think you are going to fly off the rollover of the almost-treeless slope and into the pink-and-tan Rio Grande Valley below. Also coming down from the summit, off the Tesuque Peak Chair, is **Sunset**, which leads to **Lower Burro** and back to the base. It winds its way down the mountain like a road, which it is, in fact, in the summer. Even strong beginners can handle it, allowing them to access the very summit of the mountain and its spectacular views.

Yet another run off the Tesuque chair that strong intermediates can tackle, despite its expert rating, is **Burro Alley**. One section, **Bonzai Pipeline**, is quite steep, with banked walls towering over its gut, but it is only 100 yards or so in length; the rest of the run is solid intermediate terrain. It was the very first run cut from the summit, back when the top was reached only by a giant poma. I remember being scared silly as a kid by the Pipeline section, but I could always practice my side slipping.

An intermediate run that few people find, off the Millennium chair, is **Camp Robber**. It has lots of rock and some spots are late to be buried, so keep one's speed in check here. While classed as an expert run, strong intermediates will enjoy **Parachute** on the upper mountain. Although fairly steep, it is usually well groomed and is very wide.

Expert Runs

Most of the expert runs are found on the

upper mountain, but there are a few choices off the quad chair. **Muerte** is sometimes used for ski races and has a challenging pitch but is quite wide and regularly groomed. Next to it, at the far west edge of the area, is **Desafio**, which is not groomed and therefore substantially more challenging than Muerte (and often overlooked). The top pitch on **Thunderbird** is always heavily bumped up and fairly steep. Follow it down to Crossover and then dip into the **T-Bird Trees** on skier's right. This is a shortish but excellent stash of tree skiing and powder. If you bear to skier's right you pop out on Midland and can hit the chairs to the upper mountain. Another seldom-skied expert run on the lower mountain is **Pinball**, under the old Riblet two-person chair. The moguls here get huge!

Many choices await experts on the upper mountain. Some I will cover in sections below on powder, bumps, and trees, but here are some other suggestions. **Parachute**, off the Tesuque Peak chair, is an easier expert run, as it is usually groomed. **Wizard**, also off the Tesuque chair, is another run I'd place somewhere between expert and intermediate. **Columbine** has a very steep upper entrance but you can come in from its sides at an angle and get into its center, which then becomes a relatively easy expert slope.

Powder

I'd characterize many of Ski Santa Fe's best expert runs as powder runs because they are rarely or never groomed. At the top of this list is **Cornice**. You often must ski under a rope to get to it, but this is mainly to prevent novices headed to Gay Way from getting in over their heads; the run is usually open despite the rope (check blackboard at top of the chairlift for closure notes). To get to it, start down the approach to Gay Way, then traverse hard left and out as far as you feel comfortable. The first leg might be wind scoured, but the conditions get better the farther out you go. Eventually you will find another rope, which marks the ski area's true boundary. If you ski below this, you will either have to hike back up to the run out, or commit to skiing into Big Tesuque Peak drainage, which is not advised for inexperienced skiers (see notes below on Big T). So

ski parallel to the boundary rope, which drops through glades and pocket meadows to a traverse back to the bottom of Gay Way.

Both **North Burn** and **South Burn** are also popular powder runs and can be fantastic after a big storm. However, they are susceptible to wind compaction and scouring, as they have little tree cover and so are not suitable after big winds. If you ski North Burn, angle to skier's right as the trees close in, and finish off the run on **Fall Line**, which is the old giant poma lift line. **First Tracks** is another powder haven, which in good years can lead you to the top of **Easter Bowl** and its technical entry dropping into an often-untracked field below.

Powder is almost always found in **Sunset Bowl**; come into it as high as you can through the trees from either its north or south edge.

Ski Santa Fe also has enticing out-of-bounds skiing. Some of this can kill you (as it has in the Nambé Chutes), so it's not a lark. But there are many safe and sublime lines down **Tesuque Peak**, such as Big T, as it's known, which drops you down to the ski area access road, NM 475. You can park a car at the Big Tesuque Creek pullover or just stick a thumb out from this end point of the run. I've never waited more than 20 minutes (on a weekday after lunch) for a ride. It offers about 2,250 vertical feet; its second half is largely along a narrow, dipping, bobsled-like course through an aspen forest. But don't ski this solo, or if you have not mastered deep powder skiing. It is not patrolled or groomed in any

way. You can get stuck in a terrain trap along Tesuque Creek and make other mistakes. Make a friend on the chair who knows the terrain, and don't ski it late in the day.

Bumps

Probably the best mogul run here is **Road Runner**, which drops under the Tesuque Peak chair. It is nearly straight down the fall line and can be linked to **Bozo**, which has a very steep initial pitch and big moguls. **Desafio**, on the lower mountain, is always bumped up, as is Thunderbird, and Parachute is sometimes split-groomed, so that one side has moguls and the other is smooth. One of the newest runs, **Ristra**, under the Milly chair, has very steep, moguled upper section, and Columbine is always a field of moguls. An option on the lower mountain is **Dr. Rich**.

Trees

I think Santa Fe has the best tree skiing in the state. While the woods are often impenetrable at other ski areas, Santa Fe is blessed with old-growth, mature trees in its uppermost zone, and thus the trees are well spaced and you can ski almost at will anywhere on the upper mountain.

In addition, some runs have been thinned and gladed, such as **Tequila Sunrise**, off the Tesuque Peak chair, and Cody's Glade between Avalanche Bowl and Desperado. **Lower First Tracks** is entirely in the woods, as is **Richard's Run**. The trees to skier's right of Wizard are wonderful, with a fast pitch but room to roam.

The top of **Big Rocks** also begins in nicely open trees, then tops out above a large rock-studded face that offers the most technically challenging runs on the mountain—a series of short chutes numbered 1–7. They require lots of snow to be opened, but when they are on, they are a thrill. Take care in here, as smallish cliffs can be quite tricky and potentially dangerous, and lots of huge boulders can be hidden by drifted snow.

Cruisers

Most of the lower mountain runs, like **Broadway**, **Spruce Bowl**, **Midland**, and **Open Slope** are groomed daily and make for fine cruising. But the longest cruiser here, starting from the summit, is **Gay Way**, or the combination of **Sunset** to **Lower Burro**. Neither ever gets very steep, and they offer a sustained pitch and lots of room for big GS turns.

Terrain Parks

Ski Santa Fe does not put much emphasis into

this facet of skiing or boarding but usually has a modest park functioning by mid-January. It is located off Santa Fe Trail below Gay Way.

Dining

On the Mountain

There are only a few options for eating at the ski area, as there is no base village here. **La Casa Lodge** at the bottom has a better-than-average ski area café, with a fairly wide range of options, from fresh soup, sandwiches, and salads to excellent daily specials. Between 2011 and 2013, La Casa underwent a major remodel and expansion, growing to some 30,000 square feet, including major additions to the rental shop, sport shop, and restrooms on the lower level. On the upper level, the food services, kitchen, and dining areas were also expanded, with a new menu and coffee bistro. In 2014, the facility was nominated for a national commercial development award. Brown baggers are welcome to sit inside the building and eat lunch, and its spacious, sunny deck has grilled burgers and other offerings. It is also open for breakfast, with notable burritos. There is no alcohol served here.

For spirits, you will need to head to the mid-mountain **Totemoff's**. It has a full bar and a handful of beers on tap, with an outdoor grill serving burgers, grilled chicken sandwiches, and other hot basic fare. Inside, it also serves green chile stew, excellent tamales, pizza, Frito pie, and other quick dishes, and on weekends its deck cooks up. I love Totemoff's. On its deck hang two of the original chairs from the state's first chairlift, and it offers a view of skiers descending the slopes. Inside are a fireplace, ski memorabilia, and a scattering of tables. But it is now undersized, and on peak days trying to get a beer or food can mean a really long wait. There are plans to replace the structure to increase capacity, and by the time you read this, this might have been done.

In Town

You can't shoot down to town for lunch unless you want to take hours out of your ski day, but for dinner and breakfast Santa Fe offers a tremendous range of options for every pocketbook and specialty interest. Of course, it offers great New Mexican fare smothered in red chile sauce or fresh green chile, but also all sorts of other ethnic foods, from Indian, Thai, Italian, and French to African and Japanese. It

is noted for its attention to organic and locally grown produce, dairy, and meat.

Perhaps the best New Mexican food in town is found at the **Shed** (just a half block off the Plaza at 113 Palace, 505-982-9030, https://www.facebook.com/The-Shed-of-Santa-Fe-549282815179044). Opened in 1953, it serves a delicious red chile on many of its favorite plates, and its mocha cake is to die for. Its bar is a terrific place to sneak in for a solo meal. Open for lunch and dinner, it is very popular, so expect a wait on all but the slowest days.

Casa Sena (just a block from the Plaza at 125 East Palace, 505-988-9232, www.lacasasena.com) is a real treat if you can splurge. Its adobe walls are covered with fine regional art, and the food is sure to satisfy. Elk tenderloin and other game are specialties, but there are also fresh fish, New Mexican dishes, and excellent salads on the menu, plus a selection of fine wines and cocktails.

At the other end of the price scale is **Dr. Fieldgoods** (2860 Cerrillos Road, 505-471-0043, www.drfieldgoods.com), where the young owner and staff bang out innovative entrées, sandwiches, soups, and desserts focused on organic ingredients and fresh-picked produce. Try the quinoa salad, the carne adovada egg roll, or the pork confit with fresh kale, house pickled red onions, and local meat. The restaurant is open daily for lunch and dinner.

For some of the most inventive, healthy, and delicious dishes you've ever eaten, drop by **Café Pasqual's** (just a block from the Plaza at 121 Don Gaspar, 505-983-9340, https://pasquals.com). Many a romance has been sparked at its community table, where singles are seated. Almost all the food is organic, and much is locally sourced. Its hearty breakfasts, such as corned beef hash with poached eggs, will get you rolling. Its motto, "Panza lena, corazon contento" ("Full belly, happy heart"), says it all.

For fun après-ski noshing and libations, or dinner and live, light music, visit **El Meson** (just two blocks from the Plaza at 213 Washington, 505-983-6756, www.elmeson-santafe.com). A Spanish-inspired tapas menu in the bar or full entrées in the dining room include fresh seafood, serrano ham, paella, and dishes from Andalucia, Catalonia, Madrid, and other exotic regions of Spain.

Other places to check out include **Geronimo** (high end), the **Compound** (very pricey), **Maria's** or **La Choza** (two other great New Mexican spots), **Second Street Brewery** (good pub grub and local beer), **Mu Du Noodles**, the **French Pastry Shop** (for breakfast or excellent onion soup), the **Pantry** (another good breakfast spot on Cerrillos Road), **Shoko** (oldest local sushi establishment), **India Palace**, **La Boca** (small plates), **Bouche** (fine French cuisine), **Il Piaato** (notable Italian and excellent service), **Tune Up Café** (modestly priced), the **Bull Ring** (arguably the best steaks in town), **Radish and Rye** (bourbon-paired fine dining), and **Coyote Café** (inventive and expensive).

Lodging

There are no overnight accommodations at the ski area. But the town of Santa Fe, 30 minutes away, has thousands of beds, from cozy bed-and-breakfasts and historic hotels to luxury resorts.

For bed-and-breakfasts, check into the **Inn at Vanessie** (427 West Water, just a five-minute walk to the Plaza, 505-984-1193, www.vanessiesantafe.com), which features comfortable, attractive rooms with southwestern décor, fireplaces, on-site free parking, and many other nice touches, including an adjoining piano bar and restaurant. **El Paradero** (220 West Manhattan, five blocks from the Plaza in the South Capitol District, 505-988-1177, 888-555-0918, www.elparadero.com) has about a dozen rooms; the most spacious, luxurious, and light filled are upstairs in the main house. Five miles from the Plaza on a beautiful property is **Raven's Ridge** (22B Ravens Ridge Road, 505-988-1288, www.ravensridgecasita.com), decorated with regional antiques in a contemporary setting; each room has a private patio or balcony.

La Zona Rosa at Las Palomas (460 West San Francisco, 505-982-5560, 855-982-5560, www.laspalomas) is a condo complex with many room options for large families. It is just a five-minute walk to the Plaza.

The essence of Santa Fe can be found at **La Fonda** (just steps off the Plaza at 100 East San Francisco Street, 505-982-551, www.lafonda santafe.com), the site of one of America's oldest overnight accommodations for travelers. Built in Pueblo Revival style, it is chockfull of local art, has a colorful bar with live music most nights, a fine restaurant, and an array long-standing shops. Each room is custom decorated, no two alike.

Just a few miles north of the Plaza, but out of town, is **Bishop's Lodge** (off NM 590, 505-983-6377, www.bishopslodge.com), another historic (first opened in the 1920s) first-rate resort with a charming bar, rooms with fireplaces, an on-site restaurant, horse stables, a spa, lovely gardens, and freestanding casita suites. It is scheduled to reopen in late spring 2017 after extensive renovations.

Another luxury-level property in town is **La Posada de Santa Fe** (330 East Palace, 505-986-0000, www.laposadadesantafe.com). Set on six acres just two blocks off the plaza, it features a full spa, the excellent-fine dining restaurant **Julia**, the historic **Staab House Bar**, a concierge, valet parking, a fitness center, a business center, and other amenities.

Mid-priced options include the **Inn of the Governors** (101 West Alameda, 505-982-4333) in the heart of downtown with a restaurant and bar, **Santa Fe Sage Inn** (725 Cerrillos Road, 505-982-5952) on edge of downtown, and **Garrett's Spot** (311 Old Santa Fe Trail, 505-946-0561), also in the downtown core. On the north edge of town is the **Lodge**, with dining and a bar.

As one gets farther away from the historic Plaza area, prices tend to fall. This includes the Route 66–era **Thunderbird Motel** (1821 Cerrillos Road, 505-983-4397) and the exceptional motel **El Rey Inn** (1862 Cerrillos Road, 505-982-1931, www.elreyinnsantafe.com), with a hot tub, fireplaces in some rooms, a dining room, and gardens. There are also numerous chain motels and hotels like Motel 6 and Quality Inn.

Buffalo Thunder Resort (located 15 minutes north of town off US 84/285, 505-455-5555, 877-455-7775, www.buffalothunderresort.com), a Hilton property, has a large gaming wing with the full complement of Vegas-style gambling options; a very good restaurant, **Red Sage**; and a nightclub. It offers shuttle service into town and has a full spa, a pool, and many other amenities.

Nightlife

Santa Fe is not a major center for nightlife, as its population is just not large enough, especially in fall and late spring, to support a thriving music scene. There are, however, a handful of clubs and bars that present good local and touring acts, and if one includes first-rate film venues, classical music concerts, literary lectures and book events, gallery and museum exhibition openings, and other cultural events, there's an amazing abundance of things to see and do here at night.

Perhaps the liveliest scene is found at **Skylight** (139 West San Francisco, 505-982-0775, www.skylightsantafe.com), with its wraparound upstairs balcony and mixture of DJs and local and national touring acts. Just across the street is **Evangelo's** (200 West San Francisco, www.facebook.com/Evangelos-Cocktail-Lounge-316627291684851), a stalwart of the downtown nightlife, with bars upstairs and down, and often music on weekends in both spaces. Say hola to Nick, the long-standing proprietor. **El Farol** (808 Canyon Road, 505-983-9912, www.elfarolsantafe.com), has live music most nights and is also a great spot to sample Spanish tapas and other small-plate dishes, as well as excellent entrées. The **Cowgirl** (319 Guadalupe, 505-982-2565, www.cowgirlsantafe.com), which also serves tasty comfort foods, is usually popular and packed, especially when its patio is going.

In Addition to Downhill Skiing

I just touched upon some of the non-skiing activities in Santa Fe, but that is only scratching the surface. Because of the huge elevation change between town and the ski slopes, in town one can hike (www.sfct.org/trails/dale-ball-trails or www.santafe.org/Visiting_Santa_Fe/Things_to_Do/Hiking), go horseback riding, or even—in late winter—play golf or tennis *and* ski on the same day.

Santa Fe also has more than 200 **one-of-a-kind retail shops**, more than 100 **galleries**, and three casinos—**Buffalo Thunder** (see Lodging), **Camel Rock**, and **Cities of Gold**—run by various Indian tribes just 15–20 minutes from town.

One can also sign up for cooking classes here (**Las Cosas**), take a pottery-making workshop, learn to print or paint, attend a photography clinic or other short-term arts and crafts courses.

There's also a collection of world-class museums here, including the **New Mexico Museum of Art**, the **Museum of Indian Arts and Culture**, the **Museum of Spanish Colonial Art**, the **New Mexico History Museum**, the **Museum of International Folk Art**, the **Museum of Contemporary Native Art**, and the **Wheelwright Museum of the American Indian**. For something really different and fun, visit the interactive art facility **Meow Wolf**.

Within an hour or so of town are **Pecos National Historic Park**, **Kasha-Katuwe Tent Rocks National Monument**, and **Bandelier National Monument**, as well as a handful of **Pueblo Indian communities**—including Cochiti, Tesuque, Santa Clara, and San Ildefonso—open to visitors. Santa Clara and San Ildefonso, in particular, have lots of home studios and galleries where you can view and shop for handmade pottery, jewelry, and other arts and crafts.

Something with strong appeal to tired skiers is a visit to **Ten Thousand Waves** (3451 Hyde Park Road, 505-982-9304, tenthousand waves.com), the town's Japanese-style bathhouse. It is located on the ski area access road just above town and has private and group tubs, saunas, cold plunges, and excellent massage services, plus a fantastic Japanese tavern with a small plates restaurant, **Izanami**, and exquisite overnight lodging.

For details on visiting, staying, and dining in Santa Fe, see www.santafe.org and www.santafe.com. For daily schedules of special events see the *Santa Fe New Mexican* newspaper and their fine weekly arts and culture magazine, *Pasa Tiempo* (http://www.santa fenewmexican.com/pasatiempo/), or other local periodicals.

Taos Ski Valley

Address: 116 Sutton Place, Taos Ski Valley, NM 87525

Ski Report: 866-968-7386, ext. 2202

Information: 575-776-2291

Reservations: 800-776-1111

Websites: Taos Ski Valley resort: www.skitaos.com; Village of Taos Ski Valley: www.vtsv.org; town of Taos: www.taos.org

Facebook: Taos Ski Valley

Twitter: @taosskivalley

Instagram: @skitaos

Operating Hours: 9 a.m.–4 p.m. daily

Season: Generally Thanksgiving through Easter (with occasional later openings and extended closings)

Mountain Profile

Base Elevation: 9,200 feet

Summit Elevation: hike-to 12,481 feet; lift-served 12,450 feet

Vertical Drop: 3,281 feet

Annual Snowfall: 305 inches

Area: 1,294 acres

Runs: 110 named

Longest Run: Rubezahl (5.5 miles)

Lifts: 15 (four quads, three triples, five doubles, three surface)

Lift Capacity: 15,000 skiers per hour

Terrain Classification: Beginner: 24 percent; Intermediate: 25 percent; Expert: 51 percent

Terrain Parks: Bambi Glade Beginner Park and Maxies

Snowmaking: All beginner and intermediate terrain

Seasonal Visits: 250,000 skiers per year

Backcountry Access Policy: Illegal to ski anywhere out of bounds

Season Highlights: Brew Masters Festival and Demo Days (mid-December), Taos Winter Wine Festival (second to third week in January), Rio Hondo Rando Raid Ski Mountaineering Championships (early February), Taos Freeride Championships (late February / early March), Ernie Blake's Birthday and Beer Festival (mid-March), Ben Myers Ridge-a-Thon (mid-March), and Slush Fest and Pond Skim (late March / early April)

Webcams: Several, including base and ridgeline, with viewer control

Amazing Facts: Taos helped pioneer in-bound extreme skiing in the United States. The original road to the ski area had more than a dozen in-stream crossings.

The Bottom Line: Taos Ski Valley (TSV), the largest and most renowned ski area in New Mexico, features world-class terrain and typically excellent snow in a laid-back, friendly, unconventional, and legendary culture. Known as an experts' Valhalla, it's large enough to have terrain for all levels of skiers and boarders, and it attracts an international clientele.

Getting Here

Driving

Taos is located in north-central New Mexico in the Carson National Forest, 19 miles northeast of the town of Taos, at the end of NM 150.

If coming from the north (Colorado), approach town on NM 522 and turn left (east) onto NM 150.

If coming from the east (Texas), approach town on US 64, passing Angel Fire and crossing over Palo Flechado Pass. Drive north through town on Paseo del Pueblo, and turn

Flying

The closest major airport is the **Albuquerque Sunport**, and commercial flights also land in Santa Fe. You can rent a car in town. I suggest four-wheel drive or take a paid shuttle (see below). The town of Taos recently expanded its airport and commercial carriers are now being lined up. No details were available as this went to press.

Train and Bus Links

Amtrak stops at Raton (96 miles northeast of Taos via US 64), and at Lamy (near Santa Fe).

There is also a commuter rail service, the **Rail Runner** (www.nmrailrunner.com), which operates multiple times a day from Albuquerque to downtown Santa Fe with daily service. It includes a bus link in Albuquerque to the airport, and bus service from Santa Fe to Taos (on Saturdays and Sundays only, with five round trips) called the **Taos Express**. The Taos Express operates on a first-come, first-served basis. The fee is $5 per trip. For details on the Taos Express, call 866-206-0754 or visit www.taosexpress.com.

There is also daily bus service, the **Chile Line**, running between the town of Taos and TSV from pre-Christmas through March. It runs from the Sagebrush Inn on the south side of town; it makes ten stops in town and four more stops north of town. It costs $1 per ride; exact change required. There are four round trips per day. For schedule and map of stops, call 575-613-1418 or visit www.RideTheBlue-Bus.com.

Shuttles

There are at least three shuttle services running between the Albuquerque Sunport and Taos Ski Valley.

TSV Shuttle (575-776-2291, ext. 2384, 800-776-1111, www.skitaos.com/discover-taos/airport-shuttle) departs Albuquerque for Taos daily at 12:30 and 3:30 p.m., and departs Taos for Albuquerque daily at 7:30 a.m. and 11:30 a.m. Shared rides cost at least $67 one way between Albuquerque and TSV, and at least $50 to and from Santa Fe. Reservations are required 48 hours in advance, and there is a maximum of three bags.

Twin Hearts Express (800-654-9456, 575-751-1201) provides daily service heading north

right (east) onto NM 150.

If coming from the south (Santa Fe and Albuquerque), approach town on NM 68 from Española. Drive time from Albuquerque is about three and a half hours; from Santa Fe, two and a half hours.

Additional driving directions are found on the TSV website, in the section titled "Getting to Taos."

Taos Transportation (575-776-2291, ext. 2383 or 2384, shuttle@skitaos.com) also provides door-to-door rides within Taos County at a fee of at least $75 per hour. Reservations are required at least 24 hours in advance.

from Albuquerque Sunport at 12:30 p.m., 2:30 p.m., 4:30 p.m., and 6:30 p.m. It departs TSV for Albuquerque daily at 6 a.m., 8 a.m., 10 a.m., and 12:30 p.m. The fee is about $105 round trip.

Mountain View Shuttle (575-770-8759, www.mountainviewshuttle.com) runs two to three round trips a day weekdays and three trips on weekends. Round trip costs at least $200 per person. Private cars and drivers also available.

Carpool

Another option is to carpool—a fun, cheap, and environmentally friendly way to get to the resort. Visit www.carpoolworld.com/taos to create a profile and find new friends looking to share a ride.

Maps

For an online map of the Village of Taos Ski Valley, visit www.taosskivalley.com/sites/default/files/website/161122%20Village%20Map.pdf.

Services

Lift Tickets

This is New Mexico's most expensive lift ticket, but still much more affordable compared to ski areas elsewhere in the world. Expect adult single-day tickets to cost at least $98 per day, and half day at least $84; teens

(ages 13–17) full day at least $81, and half day at least $63; children (ages 7–12) at least $61; seniors (65–79) full day at least $81, half day at least $63; free for children ages 6 and under (with a paying adult) and those 80 and older. Seniors 70–79 qualify for a discounted season pass. Beginner tickets run $50 to $20 or less, depending on age. Various multi-day and lodging/lift packages can significantly reduce costs. Groups are also provided discounts (call 575-776-2291, ext. 2360 for details). Half-day tickets begin or end at 12:30 p.m. Opening and closing weeks feature reduced prices. Reduced-cost tickets can be bought online at www.store.skitaos.com.

The Taos Card provides direct-to-lift access, $17 off the single-day ticket rate during regular season, with every seventh day free, plus discounts on food, demo rentals, tune-ups, and retail purchases. It costs at least $75, and at least $40 for kids and teens.

Taos Ski Valley is also part of the Mountain Collective, which provides two-day access to at least 14 ski resorts nationally. Visit www.mountaincollective.com for details.

It also sells a variety of season passes at a wide range of costs (from $1,100 to free), depending on your age and occupation.

The ticket office is located next to the Resort Center across the pedestrian bridge in the central base area. You can also buy tickets online in advance. For all ticket and card

details, call 866-968-7386 or e-mail tickets@ skitaos.com.

Rentals

Taos Ski Valley has numerous rental options. The resort's own shop, Taos Ski and Boot (575-776-2291, ext. 2267) rents ordinary skis (at least $33) and high-end demo skis (at least $52), plus snowboards (at least $45) and telemark skis (at least $42). Rentals include boots and poles. The rental shop will be located on the ground floor of the Blake, TSV's new slopeside lodging.

There are also a handful of private rental shops focused on higher-end rentals, plus apparel and related goods. No shop rents alpine-touring gear. Private shops include the following:

Alpine X-Treme (in the Edelweiss Hotel, 575-776-8380, www.alpinextreme.com)

The Boot Doctors, a complete ski shop and one of America's finest boot fitters (in Alpine Village, 575-776-2489, bootdoctors.com)

Cottam's Ski Shop, with free overnight storage on slopes (in Alpine Village, 575-758-2822, 800-322-8267, www.cottamsskishops.com)

Le Ski Mastery, with racing gear, technical clothing, and excellent tuning services (location shifting, 575-776-1403, www. leskimastery.com)

Terry Sports (11 Ernie Blake Road, 575-776-8292, www.terrysports.com)

Tuning

In addition to the private shops above, the official TSV rental shop, **Taos Ski and Boot** (575-776-2291, ext. 2267, in the Blake Hotel), provides a range of services for skis and snowboards.

Retail Shops

There are a growing number of shops in the base area where you can purchase winter clothing and gear, regional arts and crafts, Andean woven goods, and small gifts. Some that have been located on Thunderbird Road, which is in the process of becoming a complex of condominiums, retail shops, and places to dine and drink, will relocate, and others will move into the new facilities; exact locations are to be determined.

There's also a small grocery and convenience store, **Bumps Market** (located on the north side of the Snakedance Condominiums,

575-776-1360). It also carries beer, wine and spirits, and even oxygen bottles. It is open 8 a.m.–8 p.m.

Ski School

Taos has one of the continent's highest-rated instructional programs, the **Ernie Blake Snowsports School**. The ideal learning situation for skiers and boarders is to enroll in a Snowsports Week, which includes a morning lesson for six days with the same instructor, in small classes. But single (at least $70 for two and a half hours), two-day, and multi-day group classes are also offered at all levels, as well as private lessons (beginning at $300 for three hours). Adult telemark lessons are also every Sunday afternoon.

During peak periods there are learning groups created just for teens; one week a season is devoted to racing technique and another week devoted to "total immersion" for advanced skiers. Every winter there is also a two-day boarding "camp," two two-day camps for mastering moguls and steeps, and a two-day telemark festival with clinics.

For details or to make reservations, call 866-968-7386, ext. 2340 (or 2255 or 2256) or visit www.skitaos.com/lessons/adult.

Adaptive Ski Program

Taos Ski Valley has trained instructors who assess, equip, and teach students with disabilities in a one-on-one setting. This includes two-, three-, and four-track skiers, snowboarders, bi-skiers, and beginning to advanced mono-skiers. Lessons run from two to six hours. Reservations are required through the ski school. For details contact the private lesson desk at 575-776-2291, ext. 2355.

Childcare

Taos also has an excellent program for kids, including infants. On-snow play and instruction begin at age 3, with programs designed for teens up to age 12. Daycare is available for infants 6 weeks and older. Children even have their own ski zone with pint-sized lifts, and a rental equipment shop. Check-in for lessons begins at 8 a.m. Classes form at 9:30 a.m. On-snow pickup time is 3:15 p.m.; indoor pickup time is 3:30 p.m. The **Children's Center** is located a short drive from the main base area, on the west side of Strawberry Hill, on Firehouse Road. For details and reservations (highly recommended during peak periods), call 866-968-7386, ext. 2340 or e-mail snow sports@skitaos.com.

Mountain Tours
None

Lockers
Found on the ground floor of the Resort Center

Cell Phone Service
The resort has recently installed mobile cell towers in the valley to improve cell phone reception, and a new fiber-optic system to boost capacity, so service is now okay to excellent on the slopes (depending on exact location).

First Aid
The primary first aid / ski patrol center, also known as **Mogul Medical** (575-776-8421), is found just to the west of the Hotel St. Bernard, next to Strawberry Hill. It is open for walk-in or scheduled service 9 a.m.–4:30 p.m. daily.

On the mountain are several patrol stations, including the headquarters atop Chair 2, and at the summit of Kachina Peak.

Background

Taos Ski Valley has a character and ambience unlike any other community in New Mexico. The mystical, harshly beautiful, and haunting character of northern New Mexico pervades the craggy peaks of the Sangre de Cristo Mountains that wrap their arms around this enclave. Here one feels transported to another realm, a different time and place with an almost-magical aura.

Perhaps its charm comes from the mix of its original European founders—people like Ernie Blake, the Hotel St. Bernard owner Jean Mayer, and all the instructors and innkeepers and administrators Ernie recruited many decades ago to come to the high-desert home of Taos Pueblo Indians and Hispanic farmers and launch a ski resort. It seemed impossible then, and still improbable, that it made it. The 1960s and 1970s brought a huge influx of hippies and other seekers to the region, producing a hybrid culture like none other.

That it harbors unique people is clear. Also notable is the sheer majesty of the locale. Atop Chair 2, the world falls away in an awesome panorama of sharply etched peaks, huge bowls, and vistas of more distant mountains,

including the San Juans of Colorado, nearby Gold Hill, and the state's highest summit, Wheeler Peak. You take a big breath of the pine-scented, crisp air, steeling yourself for the drop into the massive old-growth trees of Pollux, scan the view one more time, and push off. There are new lessons and age-old truths waiting to be revealed—if you're ready.

Cut off from the surrounding high-desert terrain and tucked within the folds of the Hondo Valley, the ski area seems unusually welded to its environment. Serious skiers and lovers of high-alpine country flock here from around the world, drawn to its multicultural setting and the old-fashioned emphasis given here to the skiing rather than creature comforts or flash. Many return over the years and even generations for the incredibly light and prodigious snowfall (more than 25 feet, typically) and the challenging skiing found amid the highest peaks in the state.

With new ownership in 2014, significant improvements to the resort's infrastructure, lift system, and accommodations—including a four-star hotel that opened for the 2016–2017 season—are underway. A new block of condominiums, shops, and places to eat and imbibe is being built alongside the dashing Lake Fork Creek, significantly expanding the footprint of

the base village. In the 2014–2015 season, a new chairlift was opened on Kachina Peak, taking the resort's lift-served vertical feet of skiing to a substantial 3,250 feet and an elevation of 12,450 feet. But statistics can't capture its significance. Of course, in the past one could always make the 30- to 45-minute hike up Highline Ridge to ski the peak, but being able to do so run after run, with a mere 5-minute chair ride up, is something entirely different. In a word—exhausting!

Also rustic, TSV is a place where a hotel owner, a bartender, a daycare provider, or instructor will happily stay on board for decades and remember you from the year or years before. More so than almost any resort I've ever visited, it feels like a home away from home. And while the lifts no longer shut down for sit-down multicourse lunches, the pace does seem a little slower than at your average resort, perhaps colored by New Mexico's mañana attitude. Or maybe it's the golden sunshine that bathes these mountains in light day after day that has taken the hard edge off life and mellowed those who live, work, and visit here.

One of the nation's older ski areas, TSV was founded in 1955 by the late Swiss German Ernie Blake, his American wife, Rhoda, their children, and a handful of associates Ernie recruited from Europe to run the lodges, the ski school, and shops. People told him he was nuts to put a ski area in such a remote region studded with steep terrain, but he and Rhoda persevered. A hard worker and mercurial boss who hired and fired several people multiple times, he was also a master of media massage. His early associate at TSV, the Aleut Indian Pete Totemoff, once said of him, "Whatever Ernie was marketing, bullshit or a ski area, he could do it." He was known to answer the phone late at night, introducing himself as the janitor, and then give glowing reports about the ski area and conditions. People came, many from Chicago, in the early days via the Santa Fe Railroad's Super Chief train.

Getting in touch with the environment is the paramount principle of TSV, whose founders believed mountains have much to teach us. They also had a ball pioneering the skiing of deep powder. It falls particularly lightly here in the generally dry and high environment, vying with Utah as home of the world's finest powder.

Taos lays claim to some of the nation's most radical terrain. Indeed, 51 percent of its runs are rated expert or beyond. But because of its hefty size, it also has many, many intermediate and beginner slopes—though some visitors would eagerly tack black diamond signs on runs that Taos downplays with blue squares. Even when groomed, as they are nightly, TSV's novice and intermediate runs can offer substantial challenge. But don't be put off by the initial look from the base area up Al's Run and Snakedance—you are looking at only a fraction of its terrain.

Only 20 miles away is the funky, captivating, and thoroughly novel town of Taos, which was founded in the seventeenth century by Spanish settlers near the ancient, and still thriving, Taos Pueblo, home to Pueblo Indians. Many visitors stay in town, which offers less expensive lodging and many fine places to eat. If you are staying in TSV, you should consider venturing into town to peruse the excellent galleries, museums, and shops. However, you might find it hard to pull yourself away from the skiing. Oh well—you can always return in summer.

Mountain Highlights

Beginner Runs

Although not noted for its beginner slopes, Taos has plenty of options for those just beginning to ski or snowboard. The gentlest slopes are found in the relatively new **Pioneer** area, just to the east of the base complex, served by its own gentle chairlift. To the west is the original beginner slope known as **Strawberry Hill**. It is served by four lifts and is a broad slope with various degrees of pitch, allowing one to improve progressively. The latter is where most children ski, as it adjoins the Children's Center.

Solid beginners can also tackle at least one run on the main mountain itself, the

meandering **Whitefeather**. Its roller coaster terrain, small bowls, and forest-lined trail sections provide a wonderful variety of skiing experiences, with easy-going "detours" bypassing steeper sections. From the summit on Chairs 2 and 6—which serve up stunning views of nearby Wheeler Peak, Kachina Peak, and summits to the north—the gentle **Bambi** also provides intrepid beginners (though not true beginners) a means off the mountain, as it wanders down to the top of Whitefeather. Likewise, competent beginners can even ski on the back side on **Honeysuckle** to **Winkelreid** to **Rubezahl** to complete a circumnavigation of the resort.

Intermediate Runs

Composing a quarter of its terrain, the intermediate runs at Taos can provide access to almost all sectors of the resort, except Kachina Peak. As kids we skied **Porcupine** over and over and never tired of it. Also on the lower mountain is the exciting **Powderhorn**. Off Lift 8 is the long and steadily pitched **Lower Staffenberg**, which will allow you to get a nice rhythm going. On the back side are a handful of fine intermediate runs served by the triple chair (Lift 7), such as **Lone Star**. Be sure to head up into **Kachina Bowl** on Lift 4, which often has the best snow on the mountain. There are a handful of cruisers here guaranteed to put a smile on your face.

Expert Runs

While there are lots of options for novices and intermediates, TSV's steeps (and deeps) are really its claim to fame. Taos was one of the first, if not the first, area in the nation to encourage skiing extreme terrain, pioneering the concept of *double* black diamonds. Skiing these tight, rock-lined chutes, dropping off a cornice, blasting into some old-growth spruce, and hucking cliffs was common here long before other areas dropped the ropes on such terrain. With more than 20 named double black diamonds here, you'll never run out of challenges or good snow, as their aspect (facing direction) is all over the compass, ensuring there are almost always some freshies waiting the explorer.

Even on the original lower mountain slopes, there are a handful of really tough runs, almost always densely moguled up. **Al's** is often ranked among the nation's best, hardest runs due to its really steep start and finish studded with VW Bug–sized moguls. Next to it (skier's left) is **Inferno**, with a tricky double fall line, and its sister run, **Snakedance**, which writhes right down the mountain to the Hotel St. Bernard.

Many more expert-run descriptions can be found below in the sections on Powder, Bumps, and Trees.

Powder

A plethora of powder awaits you at Taos. All

the runs can be superb on a deep and silent day during a storm, from cruisers nicely groomed the evening before to "hero" bumps on Al's softened by a foot of fresh snow.

Sir Arnold Lunn and **Lorelei** can hide stashes long after other runs are cut up. East facing, they can quickly get cooked if the sun is out, and after a freeze it can be rough going! Another often-overlooked expert powder run is **Longhorn**, one of the mountain's original slopes. Intermediates will enjoy **West Basin**.

But, to really find oneself in the White Room, head up the bootpack to **West Basin Ridge** or **Highline Ridge**. It's hard to pick a few runs out here, as each can be a delight. But study wind and sun to make the premier selection, as they significantly affect snow conditions.

The quickest access to the goods off West Basin Ridge are the narrow chutes **Spitfire**, **Oster**, and **Fabian**. Some runs off West Basin, like **Staffenberg**, face due north, so they are the last to hold light powder. Off Highline Ridge there's the wide-open **Juarez** and **Hidalgo**—the "easiest" runs of any off of the ridges. Typically, the farther out you hike on either Highline or West Basin, the fewer tracks you'll find, as on **Twin Trees**, **Tresckow**, or **Thunderbird**. Way out on West Basin is the newly created zone called **Wild West Glade**. It is a tramp to get there, but 200 or so acres of glades are a fine reward!

But the big dog at TSV for pow has to be **Kachina Peak**. It used to require a 45-minute leg burner to reach it; now a chair opened in 2015 deposits you at 12,450 feet. Above tree line, you can ski anywhere you wish, aside from the huge rock outcroppings and cliffs. Only one run off Kachina is groomed, the primary route down the center called **Main Street**. So now one also has moguls buried under the powder, making for seriously tough skiing. Fewer people make it into adjoining **Hunziker Chute** (to skier's far right off the Kachina chair), so you can often find uncut snow here after Kachina is skied out.

Bumps

There are runs throughout the resort that are left ungroomed, or that are only occasionally groomed, where intermediates, experts, and those seeking double black bumps can go at 'em.

As mentioned just above, **Al's** is a knee and leg killer with its endless moguls, as are **Inferno** and **Spencers-Snakedance-Showdown**. **Longhorn** will also have you hunched over your poles gasping for air and looking for its terminus. **West Basin** is also a great open place to blast the bumps, especially for intermediate skiers, and truth be known, as the day ends almost all runs turn into mogul fields, and one is hard pressed to avoid them.

Trees

This is perhaps the weakest page in TSV's portfolio. But in recent years they have undertaken many glading operations and the area now has some outstanding tree skiing.

Jean's Glade on the lower mountain, and Castor and Pollux on the upper, along with the superb Walkyries Glade and Lorelei Trees (both accessed from Bambi), are all notable. Two long, dedicated tree/glade runs were cut in the early twenty-first century, Ernie's Run and North American, and in the past few years a new 200-acre sector called Wild West Glade (off West Basin Ridge, requiring a 30-minute hike-ski-hike) was thinned, offering secluded, prime tree skiing. More such projects are slated for the near future.

Cruisers

Most of TSV's intermediate runs, and a few expert slopes, are groomed every night, providing a wide range of cruiser options come morning. Check the TSV website for a list of what's been worked overnight and where the corduroy awaits.

That said, I love the long descent in mornings on Lower Stauffenberg. There are usually few people here early, and it has a nice sustained but not scary pitch that allows you to really let the skis run. On the lower mountain, Porcupine is always sweet and a nice way to ease into the day. On the back side, Honeysuckle provides a sustained run down Chair 7. Under Chair 4 look for the wide-open Shalako with Kachina Peak rising above.

Terrain Parks

Taos Ski Valley has two parks for riders of varying abilities. Bambi Progression Park, located on the front side, just off Whitefeather and Powderhorn, features a handful of

features for beginner tricksters. Maxie's Terrain Park, on the back side under Chair 7, has two parallel lines. To skier's right are some smaller jumps, rollers, and features for those just beginning to explore the freestyle terrain park. To skier's left is a larger line, including several big airs. Scattered boxes and rails catering to all ability levels help to fill out the park. It is open daily 10 a.m.–3 p.m., weather permitting.

Dining

On the Mountain

The resort has two on-mountain restaurants for easy access, the Whistle Stop (575-776-2291, ext. 2283) and the Phoenix Grill (575-776-2291, ext. 2281). The former, at the foot of Chair 6, serves salads, sandwiches, and soups in bread bowls; the latter, at the foot of Chair 4, serves cafeteria-style food, along with barbecue. A better option for lunch (or breakfast, 7:30 a.m.–10:45 a.m.) is the affordable Tenderfoot Katie's Food Court (505-776-2291, ext. 2280) in the base Resort Center, just a few steps from the chairlifts, which serves up daily specials, made-to-order options, soups, deli sandwiches, and fresh salads. Adjoining it is Rhoda's (575-776-2205), a pricier, sit-down service venue open for lunch and dinner. It offers mostly New Mexico–raised beef, Taos-raised organic vegetables, a fine wine list, and craft cocktails. It is open daily 11 a.m.–8 or 9 p.m. While technically not on the mountain, the Hotel St. Bernard Deck in the base area is also very popular for lunch, as it is just a stone's throw from the slopes and enjoys a sunny location perfect for quickly downing a Dos Equis and a green chile cheeseburger. It's a lively scene. In a similar vein, just steps from the slopes on the back side, is the Bavarian (see Lodging below).

In Town

The prime ticket for dinner in the village is the Hotel St. Bernard (575-776-2251, www.stbernardtaos.com). But because its guests come first, a seat is dependent on a vacancy, which is rare during holidays. Dinner is set around large tables, so you can mingle with visitors from around the world and enjoy elegant

meals that include soup, salad, main courses, and desserts. The food is based on French cuisine but with local modifications and creative flair derived from iconic owner/director Jean Mayer, one of TSV's true treasures.

A huge step down in price, but not character or quality, is the **Stray Dog Cantina** (105 Sutton Place, 575-776-2894, www.straydogtsv.com), open for all three meals daily. For breakfast, try the heavenly blueberry blue corn pancakes, huevos rancheros, or a delicious hand-held burrito; at lunch, a great burger or grilled chicken enchiladas smothered in red chile; at dinner, red chile–seared ahi tuna, brisket tacos, or pork mole enchiladas. Homey and relaxed, it features a full bar with killer margaritas.

The **Bavarian** (100 Kachina Road, 575-776-8020, 888-205-8020, www.skitaos.com/bavarian) is just steps from Chair 4 on the back side, making it a convenient lunch spot. But for dinner, which will set you back a bit, most clientele will need to make the ten-minute drive (four-wheel drive recommended) up-canyon from the village. With its German theme, you can savor sauerbraten, wiener schnitzel, or käsespätzle, accompanied by a selection from a fine wine list or one of the beers from

Hofbräu Haus, Andechs Brewery, or Weltenburg Brewery in Germany. Tuesday is its very popular fondue night. For those who prefer an American meal, it serves salads, sandwiches, and burgers. Lunch, in its cozy interior or on its sun-drenched deck, runs 11:30 a.m.–3:30 p.m., dinner 5:30 p.m.–8:30 p.m.

The **Pizza Shack** (6 Thunderbird Road, 575-776-8866, www.taosskivalleypizza.com) is another inexpensive option in the village, and even delivers beginning at 5 p.m. It serves salads (including a tasty Caesar), meatball subs, large portions of pasta, and a wide range of specialty pizzas with New York–style dough made daily.

The **Blonde Bear Tavern** (inside the Hotel Edelweiss Lodge, 575-776-6600, ext. 6996, www.edelweisslodgeandspa.com) is a terrific spot that many visitors overlook. It is not open for lunch but features the best après-ski menu in the village, including red chile–dusted onion rings, soup de jour, and fried meatballs, and also has a full bar and extensive wine list. For dinner, start with chile-dusted onion rings, move on to iceberg wedge salad and French beef stew, rainbow trout, or pork chops, and finish it off with a rich dessert, such as creamy ricotta cheesecake in a piñon nut crust.

Café Naranja (also in the Edelweiss, 575-737-6600, ext. 6996), is a terrific breakfast spot, serving up freshly baked pastries, oatmeal, yogurt, fresh-squeezed orange juice, a full espresso bar, and breakfast entrées including french toast and huevos rancheros.

Molly's Sweet Escape (8A Thunderbird Road, as of this writing—ultimate location to be determined, 575-741-1413, www.mollys crepes.com) is a great spot for breakfast, with excellent coffee and delicious crepes, which can be ordered with everything from blueberries and nuts to green chile.

The **Hondo Restaurant** (located inside Snakedance Condominiums, 575-776-2277, ext. 230), serves lunch and dinner.

Black Diamond Espresso (two locations—in the Resort Center and next to the Phoenix at the foot of Chair 4, 575-770-8070) is a great, super-fast option for a fresh pastry or granola, along with excellent coffee, hot chocolate, mocha, or tea. Both locations are outdoor venues, with a few nearby tables.

In Town

Taos town is a diner's delight, with a surprisingly large number of fine places to eat and new ones always popping up. A long-standing local fave, at the high end, is **Doc Martin's** (125 Paseo del Pueblo Norte, 575-758-1977, www. taosinn.com) in the historic Taos Inn. It boasts a menu running from rattlesnake to rabbit but also more mainstream and extremely well-prepared entrées. The chile relleno with goat cheese and pumpkin seeds is exceptional, as are the clams and chorizo and the braised local lamb shank. Open for lunch and dinner.

El Meze (1017 Paseo del Pueblo Norte in El Prado, 575-751-3337, www.elmeze.com) features fresh, locally inspired and gathered foods, from trout to wild mushrooms. It is fairly expensive but well worth it. From the talented hands of chef Frederick Mueller, dig into the buffalo short ribs adovada; the slow-braised beef short ribs; or the house-made pasta with local greens, garlic, and shaved Manchego cheese.

The more affordable **Love Apple** (803 Paseo del Pueblo Norte, 575-751-0050, theloveapple. net) posts a daily list of local organic farms where it obtains its fresh ingredients—including farm-fresh eggs and chicken,

buffalo, beef, and game—used to create homestyle but fine meals. Chow down on buttermilk yellow cornbread, lamb meatballs, grilled trout, antelope loin, or homemade baked tamales. Open only for dinner, it is closed Mondays and only takes cash and checks.

Orlando's (in El Prado at 1114 Don Juan Valdez Lane, 575-751-1450, www.facebook. com/OrlandosNewMexicanCafe) is a popular spot for New Mexican fare—that is, anything smothered with green or red chile. A favorite place for decades to grab breakfast has been **Michael's Kitchen** (304 Camino del Pueblo Norte, 575-758-4178, www.michaelskitchen. com), with its famed breakfast burritos.

Other recommendations: **Eske's Brew Pub** (the town's original), **Kyote Club** (with full bar), **Bent Street Deli and Café**, **Lambert's** (expensive), **Taos Pizza Outback**, and **Taos Cow** (in Arroyo Seco).

Lodging

In the Village

There's a range of accommodations in the base area, from hotels and a few bed-and-breakfasts to condominiums. All are fairly expensive, as there simply isn't an abundance of places to stay.

A new luxury hotel, the **Blake at Taos Ski Valley** (www.theblake.com), opened in February 2017 at the foot of Chair 1, with 65 rooms, 15 condos, a wine and tapas bar serving sophisticated northern New Mexican–inspired cuisine, underground parking, and a spa and fitness center with regionally inspired treatments. It is the first new significant lodging in the village in more than two decades, and the long-awaited centerpiece of the TSV's base area redevelopment. It provides a unique, inviting, and sophisticated lodging experience and is centrally located among the retail shops and dining establishments of Taos's base area. The hotel's unique architecture, design, featured artwork, service, and cuisine all spring from the fusion of the resident European, Hispanic, and Native American cultures that meet in Taos. With sustainability in mind, the hotel is LEED certified, with ground-sourced heating and cooling.

The venerable **Hotel St. Bernard** (right at the base of the resort, 112 Sutton Place, 575-776-2251, www.stbernardtaos.com), the first lodge built in the valley after it opened as a ski area, is the living heart of TSV. The hotel's round copper-covered fireplace is the eternal flame of the valley where generations of kids have warmed frosty fingers on days of raging blizzards, and couples settle into its circling chairs after dinner for a nightcap. It is the compact domain of Jean Mayer, whose French upbringing is evident in the lodge's superlative food, warm ambience, and alpine style. Rooms are small and lack TVs, but one comes here for the ski-in, ski-out convenience, the four-course meals, and the friendships you will strike up with your tablemates. Although quite expensive, it is often booked a year in advance.

The **Bavarian** (a ten-minute drive up-valley from the village, 575-776-8020, 888-205-8020, www.thebavarian.com) is another great option. Ever dream of sleeping in a small stone-and-wood lodge in the Alps, tucked in under a down quilt while a fire warmed the tiled wood stove in the corner? Here's your chance, but there are only four rooms available—including a three-bedroom suite—so reserve early!

Sierra del Sol (13 Thunderbird Road, 575-776-2981, 800-523-3954, www.sierrataos.com), the first condo project in the valley, was built in the late 1960s (my father's company supplied the lumber). It has been remodeled and updated over the years into a very comfortable and convenient place—just a few hundred yards from the base area on the bank of dancing Lake Fork Creek—to gather with friends or family. Units can be linked with common doors and accommodate one to eight people. Many rooms feature wood fireplaces and balconies, and all rooms have Wi-Fi and DIRECTV. On-site parking, a hot tub, a sauna, laundry, and other amenities are available.

Alpine Village Suites (100 Thunderbird Road, 800-576-2666, www.alpine-suites.com) is tucked into a discrete complex straddling the North Fork and Lake Fork creeks just a few minutes' walk from the slopes. It features a variety of accommodation sizes (including pet-friendly rooms and some with kitchenettes), from budget studios to nearby freestanding

cabins and chalets, along with a large outdoor hot tub, a sauna, great mountain views, free Wi-Fi, and guest ski lockers.

The **Edelweiss Lodge and Spa** (106 Sutton Place, on east side of beginner area Strawberry Hill, 800-458-8754, 575-737-6900, www.edelweisslodgeandspa.com) is an attractive, comfortable, high-end property that includes a spa offering deep-tissue massages, all-natural facials, and body scrubs. With advance reservations, it is open to the public as well (call ext. 0). The lodge has on-site underground parking, an outdoor hot tub, an exercise room, a dry sauna, private boot lockers, and complimentary ski and board valet service from the on-site Alpine Extreme ski shop.

Snakedance Condominiums (just 20 yards from Chair 1, 575-776-2277, 800-322-9815, www.snakedancecondos.com) include 1–3 bedroom units with a restaurant and bar, ski lockers, small spa, gas fireplaces, Wi-Fi, and satellite TV.

Rio Hondo Condominiums (6 Firehouse Road, 575-776-2646, 800-461-8263, riohondocondos.com) feature 2–4 bedroom options, with wood or gas fireplaces, satellite TV, a large outdoor hot tub, a sauna, and laundry facilities.

The **Amizette Inn** (on NM 150 just a few miles down-valley from the village, 800-446-8267; no website). This former nineteenth-century miners' hotel turned bed-and-breakfast on the bank of the Rio Hondo provides good cooking along with a hot tub and sauna at a reasonable price.

In Town

In town, there are many options for all price ranges. There are some exceptional bed-and-breakfasts for those who like that experience, including the **Mabel Dodge Luhan House** (240 Morada Lane, 575-758-0287, www.mabel dodgeluhan.com), the former home of the famous art patron; **Old Taos Guesthouse** (1028 Witt Road, 575-758-5448, www.oldtaos. com); and the **Taos Country Inn** (720 Karavas Road, 575-758-4900, www.taos-countryinn. com), on 22 acres of pastureland. For condos, check out **Quail Ridge** (575-776-2211, quail ridgetaos.com); on the north side of town, it's closer to the ski area. For those on a budget, a several properties and motels beckon, including the area's only hostel, the **Snowmansion** (in Arroyo Seco, about halfway to town, 575-776-8298, snowmansion.com), **Kachina Lodge** (575-758-2275) (be sure to see its Pueblo-deco coffee shop), and **El Pueblo Lodge** (575-758-8700, 800-433-9612, elpueblolodge.com).

For those ready to splurge, **El Monte Sagrado** (575-758-3502, 855-846-8267, elmonte sagrado.com) is one of the nation's finest properties, with spa facilities, a refined bar, excellent restaurant, indoor pool, lovely grounds, meeting facilities, and more. In the middle range is the historic, Pueblo-styled **Sagebrush Inn** (on the south side of town, 575-758-2254), where artist Georgia O'Keeffe spent weeks on some of her early visits to New Mexico.

Nightlife

There isn't any. Just joking, but the fact is, after tackling TSV's slopes many people here are too pooped to party at night. However, there are a few dependable spots to catch live music on weekends and all holiday nights in the village, notably the **Martini Tree** (575-776-2291, ext. 2285) in the Resort Center and the **Rathskeller** in the Hotel St. Bernard. There are a few other watering holes in the valley, such as the fun **Stray Dog Cantina**; the refined **Blonde Bear Tavern** (in the Edelweiss Lodge); the **Taos Mesa Brewing** taproom, launched in 2015; the German-themed bar at the **Bavarian**; and the bar in the **Snakedance Condominiums** (see Lodging or Dining sections for contacts).

In the town of Taos, check out the **Alley Cantina** (121 Teresina Lane, 575-758-2121, www.alleycantina.com), with live music most nights, or the **Adobe Bar** (inside the historic

Taos Inn on Paseo del Pueblo Norte, 575-758-2233, taosinn.com). Another venue that often hosts local and touring acts is the **KTAOS Solar Center** (at northeast corner of intersection of Paseo del Pueblo / US 64 and NM 150 — the Ski Valley Road, 575-758-5826, www.ktaos. com), home to the excellent solar-powered radio station KTAOS (101.9 FM). A huge addition to the region's live music and performing arts scene was the 2015 opening of **Taos Mesa Brewing** (on US 64 a few miles west of NM 522, 575-758-1900, www.taosmesabrewing. com). It has good, inexpensive food, indoor and outdoor stages, and its own line of suds. What's not to like?

In Addition To Downhill Skiing

A wonderful aspect of a vacation at TSV is the range of things one can do in addition to skiing or snowboarding, both in the village and in the nearby town of Taos.

Tubing

At the resort itself, one can spend the late afternoon on the inner-tubing hill. A short lift provides the uphill access, and clear, safe lanes for coming downhill make this appropriate for people of all ages—from grandfathers to toddlers. Located in the beginners' zone on Strawberry Hill, tubing is offered during holidays and peak periods. It is $15 for adults over 18, $10 for children ages 7–17, and free to those ages 6 and under.

Snowshoeing

For those who enjoy a quiet walk in a snowbound forest, several private companies lead snowshoe tours in the valley. With **Ride-Northside** (575-776-3233, www.RideNorthside. com), experience stunning vistas of the valley along a dashing stream while enjoying a hot beverage and Taos Mountain Energy Bars. Tours start from the Williams Lake Trailhead parking lot near the Bavarian Lodge and are designed for enthusiastic beginners and intermediates with a reasonable level of fitness. Rental snowshoes are available. Offered on select dates with advance reservations.

Taos Snowshoe Adventures (800-758-5262, www.snowshoeTaos.com) provides two-hour lessons, half-day and full-day options, plus full-moon excursions.

Snowmobiling

Guided snowmobile tours to the peaks and ridges above TSV are available through **Big Al Tours** (575-751-6051, www.bigaltsv.com); they vary in length and experience.

In Town

The town of Taos, just 30 minutes away from the ski resort, has almost-endless opportunities for non-skiing activities; in fact, its summer visitors outnumber winter. For details on Taos attractions, visit www.taos.org.

This includes **shopping** in one-of-a-kind stores and dozens of **art galleries** showing everything from spanking-new contemporary works to traditional landscapes, touring **historic sites** (particularly noteworthy are the home of explorer and scout Kit Carson, the home and studio of early Taos artist Ernest Blumenschein, and the Martinez Hacienda), and visiting the town's incredible cultural institutions, such as the **Millicent Rogers Museum**, with its exceptional collection of silver jewelry, or the **Harwood Museum**, with its large body of paintings by Taos art colony founders and more recent works.

A stop at **Taos Pueblo** is also highly recommended. A World Heritage Site, the pueblo dates back close to 1,000 years. Dubbed America's oldest condo, its adobe form rises organically almost seven stories over the sagebrush plain. Without electricity or plumbing, it exudes an ageless charm and is a great place to look for authentic handmade pottery (especially notable is its sparkly micaceous work), jewelry, wood carvings, leatherworks, and more. If you can catch one of their annual sacred, traditional ceremonial dances, you are in for a real treat! There is a substantial admission fee. For details, call 575-758-1028 or visit www.taospueblo.com.

Many people are also fascinated with the **Earthship Biotecture** (575-751-0462) project located on the west side of the Rio Grande (take US 64 west across the High Bridge, and then in a few miles look for the signs and odd structures poking from the grounds on your right). Earthships are part greenhouses and part off-grid living quarters made out of old tires rammed with dirt, recycled bottles, and other found objects. Several demonstration homes are open for tours or drop-ins.

Hiking

While TSV might be buried under five feet or more of snow, down in town—especially in late winter—trails can be snow-free and suitable for hiking or biking. Especially scenic is the **West Rim Trail** above the Rio Grande Gorge. For details, visit http://www.taosnews.com/stories/taos-news-lifestyles-spring-hiking-in-taos-rio-grande-west-rim-trail,10024.

Mineral Springs Soaking

About an hour from Taos is one of America's oldest therapeutic soaking centers, the **Ojo Caliente Mineral Springs Resort and Spa** (505-583-2233, www.ojospa.com). A few hours here—with or without optional massage treatments—will restore those wobbly legs.

There are also several au naturel **hot springs** in the Taos area free to intrepid bathers. Highly recommended are Black Rock or Manby. The latter, also known as Stagecoach Springs, is just feet from the waters of the Rio Grande. It requires a bit of a drive and a substantial hike down into the Taos Gorge. See taos.org/what-to-do/water-activities/hot-springs-by-the-rio.

Ski Cloudcroft

In addition to the state's large, midsized, and small ski areas, there is one micro-option in New Mexico—Ski Cloudcroft. Even farther south than Ski Apache, it fails to open some seasons due to lack of snow, but in a good year it attracts thousands of people from southern New Mexico and Texas. Many show up just to sled and roll around in the white stuff. As the resort's Facebook page says, "Skiers and boarders, come out, point 'em downhill, let 'em buck silky smooth snow everywhere." So, I will not treat it like the other ski areas with a full-blown profile. But here are the essential details.

It is located near the small town of Cloudcroft, in the Sacramento Mountains south of Ruidoso. It sits at a decent base elevation of 8,700, sports 25 runs (eight beginner, seven intermediate, eight advanced, and two expert), a 700-foot vertical drop, and operates on 100 acres inside a 220-acre permit boundary. Its longest trail, the beginner-level Road Runner, spans almost a mile from the summit to the base.

Opened in the 1960s, and once known as Snow Canyon Ski Area, it gets you uphill on one chair, a rope tow, and a handle tow lift. It has snowmaking that covers 10 acres in the base area, the beginner slope, and the tubing hill. Although its National Ski Patrol was disbanded, it has two medical officers on the mountain at all times.

Known for its family atmosphere and low-key, friendly vibe, it also has a good instructional program with some 16 teachers providing group and private lessons. They have a full rental shop with Burton boards and Fischer skis. Special annual events include the spring Screwy Sled Scramble (build your own and race) and the Cirque de Mardi Gras in late January.

A day lodge with an upstairs café called the **Lift House**—serving burgers, chicken strips, steak fingers, soups, burritos, and such—completes the deal. They do not serve beer and wine, but you are welcome to bring your own.

In nearby Cloudcroft, take a spin at the town ice rink. Under an arched cathedral ceiling open at each end, it's usually open mid-December through mid-February and has rental skates.

Four-and-a-half miles south of Cloudcroft on Forest Road 6563 is the **Triple M Snowplay Area**, which includes a tubing hill and snowmobile rentals.

There are a handful of places to eat and to stay in town. At **Mad Jack's** (105 James Canyon Highway / US 82, 575-682-7577, open Thursdays through Sundays), dig into the excellent barbecued meat, particularly the brisket, and sides, including a tasty mac and cheese with bacon and green chile. Another option is the **Western Restaurant** (Burro Street, 575-682-2445). Open for breakfast, its bar hosts karaoke every Friday night. For accommodations, **Spruce Cabins** (100 Lynx Avenue, 575-682-2381, 877-682-2381) is a cozy place to stay with units that include fireplaces. The **Summit Inn** (one block off US 82, 575-682-2814, 877-682-2814) features rooms with cable TV, kitchenette units with dishes and utensils, and several cottages offering more room and additional privacy.

For something really special, though a bit pricey, check into the stately property simply called the **Lodge** (One Corona Place, 800-395-6343, 575-682-2566, www.thelodgeresort.com). The Victorian-style hotel was opened in 1899 and sheltered such guests as Judy Garland, Clark Gable, and Pancho Villa (he was consulting with US military leaders). Under its four-story copper-domed observatory tower are a spa, an excellent restaurant called **Rebecca's**, and a lounge with a bar once owned by Al Capone (it was cut out and shipped west). In winter you can cross-country ski around its golf course, one of the nation's highest and oldest courses at 9,200 feet. The Lodge provides cross-country rentals and instruction.

If You Go

Address: 1920 US 82, 2 miles southeast of Cloudcroft, which is 64 miles south of Ruidoso (via US 70 and NM 244)

Information: 575-682-2333

Website: www.skicloudcroft.net, plus Facebook and Instagram profiles

Facebook: Ski Cloudcroft

Instagram: @skicloudcroft

Lift Tickets: Adult all day at least $45, juniors at least $35

Rentals: Adults at least $24 for skis, juniors at least $21, snowboards at least $32 for everyone. Rentals are also available in the town of Cloudcroft (at Busick Ski Haus, 1000 West NM 130, 575-682-2284) and High Altitude Outfitters (for winter clothing, 310 Burro Avenue, 575-682-1229).

Tuning: Their ski shop can edge, grind, and wax skis and boards.

Ski School: Beginner package (lift ticket, rentals, and instruction) at least $72; 2-hour group at least $30; private at least $60 per hour; and at least $35 per additional person. Reservations are suggested.

Tubing Pass: Adults at least $24, juniors at least $18

Part Two: Cross-Country Options

I n a state with at least 66 peaks above 10,000 feet, New Mexico is blessed with abundant terrain suitable for cross-country skiing. Although people are found after a good storm shuffling their skinny skis through the streets of Santa Fe and Taos, the higher mountains are the dependable locales for a cross-country (XC) outings. There are a few regions in particular that hold snow and have the right kind of landscape for the sport, plus one full-on commercial operation and one destination within a federal reserve with organized XC options. **Angel Fire Resort** also operates a full commercial cross-country skiing operation (see Angel Fire chapter for details).

In the northern ranges, particularly the Sangre de Cristos, good skiing can be found at high elevations as early as mid-December and as late as early June. As you head into the ranges south of I-40, snowfall tends to taper off, as do elevations, so skiing there is dependent on the year and particular site conditions.

Enchanted Forest Cross-Country Ski and Snowshoe Area

Address: Physical and mail: 29 Sangre de Cristo Drive, Red River, NM 87558

Ski Report: 575-754-6112

Information: 575-754-6112

Website: www.EnchantedForestXC.com

Facebook: EnchantedXC

Operating Hours: 9:30 a.m.–4:30 p.m.

Season: Mid-December through mid-March

Mountain Profile

Base Elevation: 9,800 feet

Summit Elevation: hike-to 10,040 feet

Vertical Drop: 240 feet

Annual Snowfall: 200 inches (estimated)

Area: 600 acres

Trails: 20.5 miles of trails groomed, most for both classic and skating style; 3 miles of trails for skiers with dogs; and 11 of snowshoe trails

Longest Trail: Northwest Passage (3.1 miles)

Lifts: None

Terrain Classification: Beginner: 35 percent; Intermediate: 55 percent; Expert, 10 percent

Snowmaking: About 15 percent of the runs

Seasonal Visits: 3,387 skiers per year

Season Highlights: The center hosts the New Mexico Cup Low 02 Challenge, a qualifying snowshoe race for national finals, every year in late January. The event also includes XC races for adults and kids. It is also home to the Just Desserts event, where you ski out to enjoy sweet treats prepared by local restaurants and businesses. It is usually held in February.

Webcams: One

Amazing Facts: It boasts one of the nation's highest base elevations for a commercial cross-country ski area, 9,800 feet.

The Bottom Line: Enchanted Forest is a great addition to New Mexico's ski community, with a friendly vibe, fine range of trails with appeal to every type of Nordic skier, some sublime views, and typically adequate snowfall.

Getting Here

Driving

The ski area is located on Bobcat Pass just southeast of Red River within the Carson

National Forest. Follow driving directions to get to Red River. Then, from Red River, head southeast out of town on NM 38 for three-and-a-half miles. Just past mile marker 16, turn right onto a dirt road that climbs a short but steep, shaded hill to reach the resort—four-wheel drive is recommended. There is also

Rentals

The area's base building provides rentals. Skis, boots, and poles for a full day cost at least $16 for adults, at least $13 for a half day; teens (age 13–17) and seniors (62 and older) at least $13 for a full day and at least $10 for a half day; kids at least $8 for a full day and at least $6 for a half day. Snowshoes cost at least $13 for a full day. High-performance Fischer skis and longer backcountry snowshoes are also available for an additional $6. They also rent small, covered sleds called pulks for towing a small child; they cost at least $16 for a full day or at least $3.50 per hour.

Tuning

None

Retail Shops

The base facility also sells a limited range of essentials and accessories, plus some logo merchandise.

Ski School

Enchanted Forest offers lessons with PSIA-certified instructors to anyone from first-timers to experts. The most affordable deal for beginners includes rental boots, skis, and poles, plus 60–90 minutes of lessons and a trail pass. For adults this costs at least $45, for seniors and teens at least $40, and kids at least $35. Afternoon sessions are a bit cheaper. Morning classes begin at 10 a.m., afternoon classes at 1:30 p.m. If renting gear, arrive at least 30 minutes before your class starts.

Intermediate sessions and freestyle instruction (if you bring your own gear) cost at least $25 for one hour. A one-hour private lesson runs at least $50 (and $25 per additional person). Half-hour intensives for experts on topics like "Mastering the Backcountry" cost at least $30. They also occasionally present waxing clinics.

Adaptive Ski Program

None

Childcare

None

Mountain Tours

None

parking along NM 38, and it is just a short walk from here to the facilities, or you can call the area for shuttle service.

Flying

See chapter on Red River.

Train and Bus Links

See chapter on Red River.

Services

Trail Passes

Adult (18 years and up) all-day trail pass costs at least $18, half day (afternoons only) at least $14; teens (13–17) full day at least $15, half day at least $12; children (ages 6–12) all day at least $9, half day at least $6; seniors (ages 62–69) full day at least $15, half day at least $12. Kids (under 6) and seniors (ages 70 and up) are free.

Lockers

Found in the base building

Cell Phone Service

Spotty

First Aid

Located in the base facility

Grooming

Staff groom after every significant snowfall, and they groom some trails every day. The grooming machine lays down a nice set of tracks for traditional stride skiers and a wide, flat surface for skate skiers.

Snowshoe Tours

Two-hour guided snowshoeing tours on Saturdays include details on local flora, fauna, and landmarks. They can also be arranged on other days with advance notice, as can all-day tours with lunch. For details, call Barbara Dry at 575-754-3364.

Background

As we slipped silently through the thick forest of Engelmann spruce, Douglas fir, blue spruce, and aspen under a brilliant sun, concepts about cross-country skiing and life drifted through my head: it's all about conserving energy, using your forward kick to glide just as far as possible before another firm, steady kick. Use momentum to your advantage, what physics and conditions give you. Take what gravity delivers, but slow and steady wins the race; crashing and burning await the impatient and pushy. Breathe. Enjoy the glide. Smile. Savor this time on Earth, this wind-whipped afternoon. Sit on a grassy hillside under bristlecone pines munching on nuts and gaze out on a breathtaking expanse of northern New Mexico, from the glinting summit of Wheeler Peak to the broad white shoulder of Gold Hill and the impressive Latir Peaks. And then slip, slide, and glide back along solitary trails to your starting point, intact, tired, but renewed.

This is the experience to be had at Enchanted Forest Cross-Country Ski and Snowshoe Area, just outside of Red River, which was launched in the winter of 1985–1986 by Judy and John Miller. Members of the New Mexico Ski Hall of Fame, they are now in their eighties but still show up almost every winter afternoon to check things out and get some exercise. The business is now owned by their daughter, Ellen Goins, and is run by a mixture

of decades-old employees, family members, and new recruits. (Note: as this goes to press, the operation is up for sale.)

"We went out to visit Royal Gorge in California (a long-established XC center) and found it to be such a lovely place," explains Judy Miller, "that we decided to come back and start our own operation. John had grown up here and knew about this area and its old logging and mining roads." They began with a dream on a shoestring budget but have since created the state's only commercial XC area, with all the amenities of much larger operations found out-of-state. "It's been a labor of love," notes John Miller. "In a good winter you do all right; in a bad year you lose your shirt. Grooming is expensive—and insurance."

Playing a central role in its success today is general manager Mike Ritterhouse. He has worked at the area in a variety of capacities since 2009, in addition to having been a ski patroller at Red River and Angel Fire. "It's a special, special cross-country ski area," says Ritterhouse. "We run the full gamut of skiers, from people barely skooching along on their old wood skis, to racers on the newest gear, and backcountry skiers. It's an interesting and diverse crowd. We even have people who come here annually from around the country and an occasional international visitor."

The area is the home terrain for the University of New Mexico cross-country ski team and for many years hosted a collegiate meet here that included top skiers from across the west. "We are an international destination," he says. "Our relationship with UNM has helped in that regard. During holidays and special events you will hear all kinds of languages being spoken."

The area is also popular with snowshoers, including those into racing. One of the nation's top competitors, Laurie Lambert of Austin, Texas, and Red River, trains here, and the area hosts a few major winter festival and race events. You can also sign up for guided snowshoe tours with a local naturalist, who will point out landmarks and identify flora and animal tracks etched in the snow.

Mountain Highlights

Beginner Trails

There's a batch of trails suitable for beginners here. The easiest are also those that double as the area's trails designated for skiers with dogs, including the circular path around **Grand Meadow** to the south of the base facility.

To the north in the prime skiing area is **Powderpuff**, which winds its way up small hills and across flats for two miles or more, making for a nice outing. At **Sherwood Forest**, brave skiers might turn directly north and slide out a half mile farther on this intermediate-rated trail to a great viewpoint overlooking Gold Hill.

Intrepid beginners can even access the outback warming hut at the intersection of Sherwood Forest and Sven Wiik.

Intermediate Trails

Intermediates will love the abundant gentle hills and rolling terrain of Enchanted Forest. Except for a few short, steeper passages, intermediates can even easily ski out to the far point of the area and the Northwest Passage yurt, with its tremendous views of Wheeler Peak, Gold Hill, and the upper Red River Valley.

You can cruise from side to side here as well, using the many linking spurs to create endless loops. One of the most sustained intermediate trails is **Jabberwocky**, which curls along the west edge of the area. Returning to the base, it provides a long, easy descent.

Expert Trails

Only 10 percent of the trails here are designated as expert or most difficult, but they dish up a dose of challenge, especially in a good year when pitches like **Judy's Lead** are open. Both of these trails drop off the central plateau and into a canyon on the east side of the area. It is best skied by folks on telly gear. Another

tricky trail is **Wonderland** off Long John and **Molly B. Denim** in the southeast portion of the area.

Dining

You can eat your brown-bag lunch in the base facility dining area. Discussions are underway about providing food services, but you should check on availability before arrival. For other places to eat nearby, see the chapter on Red River.

Lodging

There are at least two yurts—round, soft-walled but cozy and solid structures—equipped with propane stoves, cooking gear, wood-burning stoves, gas lanterns, beds, dining tables, chairs, and other gear available for overnight stays. One yurt has beds for eight people, the other beds for five. You need to bring your own sleeping bag. One yurt is located one mile from the base facility; another is two miles out. For a small additional fee, you can arrange for your overnight gear to be delivered to the site. No pets allowed. Most weekends are booked by late November, so book early. Weekdays are often available on a last-minute basis. Rates vary by yurt and dates, but they run at least $65 to at least $150.

For other lodging options, see the chapter on Red River.

Valles Caldera National Preserve

Although this is a commercial operation, it is run on a nonprofit basis within a federal reserve and does not compare to the level of service found at Enchanted Forest or the operation at Angel Fire.

The Valles Caldera National Preserve in the heart of the Jemez Mountains is one of the state's most beautiful spots. The immense round basin is the bottom of a collapsed super volcano's magma chamber, with high walls encircling it and a grassy interior punctured by later, smaller eruptions. In summer it is eye dazzling in its greens; in winter it rests under a blanket of white. One's sense of scale is blown here, until you spot some of its thousands of elk looking like pinpricks in its Serengeti-like plains.

The preserve has a large trail system open to cross-country skiers and snowshoers. Depending on staffing, some seven miles are periodically groomed (but classic track set only on a few trails). There are additional routes—including roads closed to winter traffic—where you will be breaking trail.

There are no rentals available here, so you will need to bring all ski gear. Talk with park rangers before you leave on any outing. Some areas might be closed to skiing or snowshoeing to protect wildlife. And come prepared for serious cold and inclement weather, with water, snacks, fire tools, extra clothing, and so on. Cell coverage here is very spotty.

To get to the preserve, from Santa Fe head north out of town on US 84/285 16 miles to Pojoaque and turn left (west) onto NM 502 (Los Alamos / Bandelier National Monument exit). Proceed eight miles to NM 4 and turn south (left). You'll pass by the entrance to Bandelier National Monument. The road then begins miles of steep climbs and sharp corners, which in winter can be a very tricky (four-wheel drive is highly recommended in inclement weather). At mile marker 39.2, turn into the preserve's main entrance road and proceed to the visitor center. The preserve road itself is plowed. All visitors must first check in at the Visitor Center.

If driving from Albuquerque, take I-25 north to the Bernalillo exit and turn onto NM 550. In San Ysidro, take NM 4 north past Jemez Pueblo and Jemez Springs. The preserve is about 22 miles north of Jemez Springs. Look for the main gate at mile marker 39.2. Travel time is about two hours from Albuquerque.

The ski and snowshoe season usually lasts from mid-November to mid-March. Admission costs at least $20 per vehicle (no per person charges). For further details, write PO Box 359, Jemez Springs, NM 87025, call 575-829-4100 (option 3 for current snow conditions) or visit www.nps.gov/vall.

Vermejo Park Ranch

This exclusive, isolated property near Raton is an option for XC enthusiasts with deep pockets. The 585,000-acre property, owned by Ted Turner and operated primarily as a hunting and fishing preserve, bristles with 12,000-foot-plus peaks, plunging valleys, well-watered streams, and world-class big game. Sprawling over the New Mexico–Colorado border and five life zones, it is operated as a guest ranch with a firm conservation emphasis. Since 1996, Turner has spent millions restoring this property to its prehistoric ecological conditions.

Booked solidly during summer, the ranch is now developing as a winter destination, with excellent ice fishing and cross-country skiing. All activities are conducted with personal guides, with accommodations in the ranch's historic grand lodges and casitas.

Casa Grande was built in 1909–1910 by Chicago commodities broker William Bartlett, and it flanks a massive log cabin structure and another smaller stone house, Casa Minor. It features a dining table accommodating 16 people, a walk-in fireplace, trophy animals on the walls, and the stuffed MGM lion—a relic of the days when Cecil B. DeMille, Douglas Fairbanks, Mary Pickford, and other Hollywood elites, as well as Herbert Hoover, F. W. Kellogg, Harry Chandler, Harvey Firestone, and Andrew Mellon, gathered here. Italian marble columns shipped across the Atlantic, rare

crystal, acres of bookshelves, blue ottomans, and Western art provide a regal touch.

The skiing terrain takes in views of nearby Culebra Peak (14,049 feet) in Colorado, immense valleys, and quiet forests of aspen and conifers. The drive from the lodging to the ski terrain might include close views of mule deer, elk, and dozens of bald and golden eagles.

Day rates, including all meals and beverages and all activities and guides, run at least $550 per person per night. For additional details, call 575-455-2059 or visit www.vermejo parkranch.com.

Ghost Ranch

Yet another possibility is to sign up for one of the several cross-country ski weekends presented at the educational, recreational, and spiritual retreat center, Ghost Ranch—located about 90 minutes northwest of Santa Fe near Abiquiu. The package includes accommodations, food, and guides, and costs at least $350 per person (double occupancy). For details, call 505-685-1000 or visit www.ghostranch. org.

Chama Area

In Chama the snow sits three feet deep on tops of snow-covered homes, with fangy, four-foot icicles hanging from second-story roofs. Six-foot piles of snow alongside streets screen the houses, and over the valley thick, gray clouds swirl and descend, spitting more snow.

This is the scene that often greets visitors at this isolated outpost on the New Mexico–Colorado frontier. Way popular in the summer for its historic narrow-gauge railroad, the wind blows cold and hard in the dark days of January, and with its sidewalks under drifts, most downtown shops and restaurants are closed. You have to admire the spirit of the people here, many of whom are working to transform its winter somnolence into white gold.

One such stalwart is Mary Ann DeBoer, chief organizer of the state's largest festival for XC enthusiasts, the Chama Chile Ski Classic. "You gotta like the outdoors to live here—and love winter," she notes. "We want this area to be considered a major destination for cross-country skiing. It's not fancy like some others, but it's got great backcountry terrain

and we always have decent to excellent snow, even in a bad snow year."

Just north of town rears a ridge of the mighty San Juan Range, its tops scraping over 12,000 feet along the Continental Divide. Always New Mexico's wettest summer spot, Chama in good years also enjoys exceptional snowfall. A visit here is truly a visit to the White World.

The Chama Chile Ski Classic

The Chama Chile Ski Classic was launched in 1973 and has grown into a nine-day extravaganza of races (classic and skating), from sprints to 18ks, as well as snowshoe races, snow-bike races, live music at night, clinics and guided backcountry outings, and snowshoe tours. The event typically attracts more than 200 competitors and more spectators from New Mexico, Colorado, Arizona, Utah, and even farther afield. On one day contestants are encouraged to show up in costume, and you might encounter some bees, a fly, or an alien buzzing about on very skinny skis.

Kids build outstanding snow towers with colored ice block windows, and the food truck dishes up Frito pies. It is usually held in mid-January.

The races are held 12 miles north of town on Cumbres Pass just off NM 17. The course is only groomed for the event's two weekends, but even the edge of town offers spectacular terrain for XC jaunts and snowshoeing. The Sargent Wildlife Area on the town's north side (take Pine Avenue / NM 29 one mile to the parking area) has marked trails rolling out into a vast treeless valley. For guided snowshoe or XC outings here, contact Cathy Bear of the **Chama Valley Outdoor Club** (www.sites.google.com/site/chamavalleyoutdoors). And for those willing to break trail, there are endless possible outings off NM 17.

Chama is also home to two sets of backcountry yurts that allow for overnight cross-country and alpine-touring trips. See Backcountry chapter for details.

The town is also a leading center for snowmobiling. Numerous companies can take you out on guided expeditions lasting a few hours to all day, from rolling meadows to advanced terrain. One notable company is **Cumbres Adventure Tours** (866-768-2131, 719-376-2161, www.cumbresadventuretours.com).

Chama is 137 miles northwest of Santa Fe, via NM 84. There are limited options for winter lodging, including a handful of motels, the old (built in 1881!) **Foster Hotel** (575-756-2296), and condos. A noteworthy option is the **Gandy Dancer** bed-and-breakfast, with an outdoor hot tub and excellent breakfasts (575-756-2191, www.GandyDancerBandB.com). Winter dining options are also limited but include the **High Country** (with attached, rockin' saloon; 575-756-2384), the Foster Hotel, the **Elk Horn Café** (south side; 575-756-2229), and a pizza parlor.

For details on Chama, visit www.chamavillage.com or www.chamavalley.com. For details on the Chama Chile Ski Classic, visit www.skichama.com.

Santa Fe Area

Located just below Ski Santa Fe, the **Norski Trail** is a convenient place to go cross-country skiing when visiting here. Although there are some moderately pitched sections, the trail is

relatively level and suitable for beginners as well as experienced skiers. The outside loop runs two-and-a-half miles. Beginners can use cutoffs to reduce the length and avoid difficult sections, and faster and more experienced skiers can lap around on various loops winding through a mixed conifer and aspen forest.

The trailhead is on NM 475, just a mile below Ski Santa Fe. It is well marked but not regularly groomed. Snowshoeing is discouraged on the trail to preserve Nordic ski tracks.

Another popular outing is the **Aspen Vista Trail**, a service road that winds to the top of Tesuque Peak from Aspen Vista, a parking and scenic point located on NM 475 (just below mile marker 14). The road, closed to vehicles, runs 5.6 miles to the summit's communication towers, climbing from 9,700 to 12,040 feet. You can go out and turn around at any point and backtrack, or you can sample the sublime aspen forest flanking the road.

Another popular option is **Pacheco Canyon Road** (Forest Road 102, also closed in winter), which descends from NM 475 to the village of Tesuque. Drive to its top, where it intersects the ski area road (NM 475), a mile above the Big Tesuque Campground, and ski down and then climb back up. There are also trails and open tree skiing in the aspen and mixed conifers at Big Tesuque Campground, which usually has ample parking.

Black Canyon Campground, located within Hyde State Park (day-use fees apply) right on NM 475 just ten minutes from town, is the lowest elevation site for Nordic skiing or snowshoeing in the Santa Fe area. Due to its lower elevation, snow is less dependable, but in a good winter it can be very enjoyable. There is a hiking trail at the rear of the camping area (closed in winter) that winds up in a small drainage that tops out overlooking the closed Santa Fe city watershed.

Jemez Mountains

While the Sangres might be considered a "male" range—pointy, hard, and proud—the Jemez to their west could be considered a female range: all eroded curves, soft contours, and a warming skin of conifers. In other words, this is excellent XC terrain.

There are hundreds of possible routes and outings, including groomed but mostly unmaintained trails, more than I can detail. But here's the broad picture.

The **Pajarito Nordic Ski Trail** sits above the city of Los Alamos, right next to the Pajarito ski area (see that chapter for access details) at the end of the Camp May Road. The main ski trail climbs through a mixed conifer forest for three miles (one way), and in good snow years additional trails open. The system is groomed for both classic and skating skiers by the hard-working members of the Southwest Nordic Ski Club, under an agreement with the US Forest Service. It is the only groomed noncommercial Nordic ski trail in the state that is free for all to use. Snowshoeing is allowed on designated trails. To check current conditions, visit the club's website (www.swnskiclub.org).

Within the Jemez Ranger District are three

sets of trails. The **Los Griegos Trails** are located about 4.6 miles west of the entrance to the Valle Caldera National Preserve (see above). The **Peralta Canyon Trails** are located about one and a half miles west of the entrance to the Valle Caldera National Preserve. The popular **East Fork Trails** are reached via a closed gate on NM 4 midway between the Redondo Campground and the Jemez Falls Campground.

The central Jemez has been explored on skinny skis since the early 1970s. Classic Jemez ski tours over the years include the San Antonio Hot Springs, Griegos Peak, Del Norte Canyon, Road Canyon, and Cerro Medio.

Within the Cuba and Coyote Ranger Districts are more options. The southern and eastern boundaries of the **San Pedro Parks Wilderness** have relatively gentle slopes, making great areas for snowshoeing and cross-country skiing. The best winter access is via paved NM 126 east out of Cuba to Forest Road 70. Forest Road 70 is frequently not passable during winter, so you likely should gear up near this intersection. It is approximately three miles to the San Gregorio Trailhead on Forest Road 70.

Unpaved Forest Road 103 leaves NM 96 between Coyote and Gallina, and it is frequently not passable during winter for highway vehicles. Embark on Forest Road 103 as conditions permit for snowshoeing and cross-country skiing.

Taos Area

Three US Forest Service (USFS) Ranger Districts—Camino Real, Tres Piedras, and Questa—surrounding the town of Taos is rich in its XC possibilities, with generally more snow than the Jemez or Santa Fe areas. The USFS website provides details on more than 65 possible snowshoe and XC skiing routes. Some of these are very arduous and require advanced skiing and logistical skills.

Note also that some trails are shared by cross-country skiers and snowmobilers, while others are designated for skiers only and still others for snowmobiles only. Restrictions are generally posted at trailheads, but you can

check with local district ranger stations for details, or visit www.fs.usda.gov/activity/carson/recreation/wintersports.

One of the easier, close to town, and popular spots is the **South Boundary Trail**. It has multiple loop and point-to-point options that take you across ridges, valleys, and peaks through conifer and great aspen stands. The trail (#64) begins at El Nogal Picnic Area on US 64 about three miles east of Taos.

Just west of town, after a solid snowfall, try the **West Rim Trail**. It serves up amazing views of the Rio Grande Gorge at your feet and the mighty Sangre de Cristos rising to the east. For details, see http://www.taosnews.com/news/taos-news-lifestyles-spring-hiking-in-taos-r-o-grande/article_8a4f6b4f-37b4-5482-8b6e-c053207d1149.html.

Amole Canyon, located about 16 miles south of Taos on NM 518, shelters an abundance of trails groomed intermittently for cross-country skiing by the Taos Nordic Ski Club. There are eight marked trails with a total length of 20 miles and range in difficulty from easiest to most difficult. The trails are at 8,100 feet, so there are generally good snow conditions all winter. For details, call 505-587-2255 or visit the USFS Ranger Station in Penasco.

The high country around Taos Ski Valley also has many trails for hardy XC skiers. See Alpine Touring section for details.

Albuquerque Area

The Sandia Mountains, which break above Albuquerque's eastern skyline like a stone wave, are an excellent place to cross-country ski in a good winter. At elevations above 9,000 feet, the snow is generally good to excellent in the woods but can be icy, crusty, and windblown in open areas and wherever the sun hits.

Many ungroomed trails within the Cibola National Forest are accessible on the Sandia Crest Highway (NM 536—see Sandia Peak ski area chapter for driving directions) and its summit parking lot. The trail system can also be reached from the top of the Sandia Peak Tramway (details in Sandia Peak chapter). Trails vary from easygoing to very steep, and conditions can vary widely, as mentioned above. Trail/parking permits ($3) can be purchased on-site. Maps are available at the ranger station in Tijeras. For questions and trail conditions, consult the Sandia ranger office (505-281-3304, www.fs.usda.gov/cibola).

Other Options Statewide

Other obscure northern ranges, such as the rarely visited **Chuska Mountains** in northwestern New Mexico on the Navajo reservation along the Arizona border, harbor enough altitude, hiking trails, and closed forest roads, along with plenty of solitude, for cross-country outings. Intrepid, well-organized cross-country parties ski in the **Brazos Mountains** high country off US 64 between Tres Piedras and Tierra Amarilla.

The **Mount Taylor / Grants** area in western New Mexico also has solid XC adventure awaiting, including an eight-mile loop route that climbs from 9,800 feet to 11,300 feet. North of Taos and Questa lies the vast **Valle Vidal**, with immense meadows and bristlecone pines. Closed winter roads require long approaches.

The southern ranges south of I-40 also hold XC options, including routes in the **San Mateos**, **Sacramentos**, and several Gila ranges—particularly in the **Black Range**.

Resources

The New Mexico Cross Country Ski Club, a membership organization based in Albuquerque, is a good source of information for options throughout the state. They also organize small group day outings, which are open to prospective members on a shared-cost basis, as well as multi-day road trips. Annual dues are $20 per person.

If you can find a used copy of the book *Cross-Country Skiing in Northern New Mexico*, snag it. Published in 1986 by Kay Matthews and Acequia Madre Press, it is out of print but is an excellent source of information about all these routes and more. It includes maps and detailed route-finding directions.

The US Forest Service also provides lots of details on XC skiing in New Mexico national forests, including the Carson (112 Cruz Alta Road, Taos, 575-758-6200), the Santa Fe (11 Forest Lane, Santa Fe, 505-438-5300), and the Cibola (2113 Osuna Road NE, Albuquerque, 505-346-3900). In addition to the main headquarters, contact the following districts:

Camino Real: Penasco, 575-587-2255
Tres Piedras: 575-758-8678
Mount Taylor: 204 Smokey Circle, Grants, 575-876-2366
Jemez: 51 Woodsy Lane, Jemez Springs, 575-829-3535
Questa: Questa, 575-586-0520
Sandia: 11716 NM 337, Tijeras, 505-281-3304
Cuba: NM 550, Cuba, 575-289-3264
Pecos: NM 63, Pecos, 505-757-6121

Part Three: Alpine Touring / Backcountry Skiing

Alpine touring (AT), also called backcountry skiing/riding or randonee, is found in a surprisingly large swath of New Mexico's high country. With some 61 peaks over 12,000 feet in elevation, and seven topping 13,000, a wealth of opportunities exist for getting *way* off the beaten track in north-central New Mexico's Sangre de Cristo Mountains.

This is where the Rocky Mountains begin, so it's a rugged and precipitous alpine environment, with massive cliffs cut by steep chutes, glacial cirques, couloirs, and terminal moraine pitches. Large portions have yet to been skied, attesting to Nuevo Mexico's many unknown qualities.

In winter it can also become a killing zone. The chutes and wind-lipped ridge-line cornices have produced avalanches that have taken lives, and others caught out overnight have frozen to death. So, if you go, make sure you know what you are doing. Be prepared with the right clothing and gear, and strong knowledge of reading the inscrutable Continental snowpack and recognizing avalanche dangers. The safest period is in spring, usually in late April through mid- to late May when the snowpack has consolidated. Ideally, go with a local who knows the terrain and is familiar with the conditions.

Santa Fe Area

In December 2015, professional skiers Lynsey Dyer and Caroline Gleich, plus Santa Fean Jamie Autumn and other female skiers, gathered to ski Lake Peak above Santa Fe, shooting videos and stills for *Skiing*. They were amazed to find what were then the best conditions in the continent, during that year's strong start of El Niño, on a range most had never heard of.

Access to **Lake Peak** (12,408 feet), **Penitente Peak** (12,249 feet), and associated runs and zones is through the ski area of Ski Santa Fe. Its parking lot at 10,350 feet gives you a leg up on the high country, and the ski area allows "uphill" skiers to use its slopes to reach the wilderness. See their uphill policy on their website (www.skisantafe.com).

Below Lake Peak, on its north face, lies a series of tree runs, open bowls, and cliff drops known as the **Nambé Cirque**. They have been named: from skier's right and arching around, they include Heaven Hill, Gulp, Valhalla, Virvana, Styx, Rubicon, Armageddon, Charon, and Acheron. Others use a numbering system of Nambé Chutes 1–8, plus negative 1 through negative 5. In this system, one popular run, Boot Out, is N2. N8 is also known as Blow Lunch; Valhalla is N4 (or Too Late); Rubicon also goes by Gladfelter's Gelande, Boot Out Chute, or N1. Whatever their names,

they provide some 700–1,800 vertical feet of descent, with summit angles pushing 40 degrees and flattening at the bottoms. You can boot back to the ridge or take a much longer but pretty route out via the Winsor Trail.

To the north of the ski area stands the summit that dominates Santa Fe's skyline, **Santa Fe Baldy** (12,622 feet). You can reach its foot at Puerto Nambé from the ski area, via the **Winsor Trail** (#254) to the **Skyline Trail** (#251). It is about a 14-mile round trip, with an elevation gain of 3,400 feet. You can go out and camp and ski numerous lines off Baldy's west or steeper east and northeast faces.

Just down the road from the ski area is a more popular spot for backcountry skiing or riding. Entirely in forests or glades, it is less precipitous than the higher country described above—and avalanche free. Parking is found off the ski area access road, NM 58 (just below mile marker 14), at **Aspen Vista**. You head out on a closed service road that slowly climbs across the lower reaches of Tesuque Peak, then begins to switchback up it. You can go clear to the radio towers on the summit, but most people choose to drop into the Tesuque's upper basin or to ski in the aspen forest that leads you gently down to another parking area at Big Tesuque Creek. Ideally you've parked a second car here, or you can hitch back up to your auto.

Taos Area

The 12,000- and 13,000-foot-high peaks near Taos Ski Valley are New Mexico's backcountry skiing loci. The ski valley makes for a great jumping-off point to dozens of high peaks and long ridgelines threaded with chutes and broad aprons—much of it above tree line. Most of the sustained pitches run about 700 to 1,200 vertical feet, but some lines deliver up to 2,000 vertical feet or more. It is accessed via the **Lake Williams Trail**.

To access the trailhead, from the Taos Ski Valley parking lot's northeast corner, drive some two miles up Twining Road to the Bavarian Lodge. This dirt road has a few fairly steep pitches, but normal passenger cars will be okay as long as the road is snow and ice free. Park in the large parking lot just below the lodge, and follow a well-beaten path heading south from the southwest corner of the parking lot. You will pass the lodge and the bottom of Chair 4. In early to midspring, this is generally where you can start skiing. The start of the Williams Lake Trail is just above a small shack called Black Diamond Espresso. From here it is about four-and-a-half miles up along Lake Fork Creek to Williams Lake. From Williams many options open up, including Wheeler Peak (13,161 feet), the state's highest point; Kachina Peak (12,485 feet); Lake Fork Peak (12,881 feet); Sin Nombre (12,819 feet); Mount Walter (13,133 feet); Old Mike (13,113 feet); and others.

Just on Wheeler alone, named runs include the Fingers (Bong Chute, Peace Sign, Middle Finger, Ring Finger, and Pinky), as well as lines on the southwest face. Strong skiers can top out on Lake Peak in three hours or so from the parking lot or slightly more to summit Wheeler.

Taos Ski Valley is also the jump-in point to a rental yurt (round, canvas-covered structures of Mongolian origin with raised wooden floors) located two miles from the northeast corner of the Taos Ski Valley parking lot. **Trail 90** along the upper Rio Hondo

Chama Area

The Chama area is mostly favored by cross-country skiers working the meadows and low-angle foothills but also includes almost-endless terrain for steep, if shortish, runs for AT skiers, snowboarders with split boards, and telemarkers willing to climb. This steeper terrain suitable for downhill skiing is found north of town on either side of NM/CO 17 around Cumbres Pass (10,022 feet).

Chama is also home to two sets of backcountry yurts that allow for overnight cross-country and alpine-touring trips. Amid dark forests of spruce and aspen, sunlit meadows, and towering peaks, it's a place few people visit in summer, and even fewer visit in the depths of winter, when temperatures commonly reach below zero and the snow buries the frozen land. Scattered across this beautiful landscape are four yurts owned and operated by Doug MacLennan and his company, **Southwest Nordic Center**. The yurts provide skiers with secure and comfortable refuges from which to explore this winter wilderness. Linked by trails, some lie in close proximity to excellent steep, open terrain.

Since establishing his first yurt in 1987, MacLennan has carefully marked all the routes with blue-painted plywood squares tied to tree limbs and six-foot poles driven into the snow-packed meadows. In the woods, trails made by previous skiers are usually discernible, but on the windswept meadow bottoms, trails are often obliterated for lengthy sections, so route-finding skills are needed. I once visited the Grouse Creek Yurt, which required a four-mile ski in and a climb of 1,000 vertical feet. That doesn't sound like much, but as afternoon temperatures fell to 20 degrees, we all whooped with joy when at last we rounded a bend and spotted the yurt sitting at the edge of a meadow, its pointed top barely protruding above the snow.

"People are often fooled by how much effort it takes to cover such distances carrying a pack," notes MacLennan. Indeed. We were pooped, but we quickly had a fire going in the yurt's excellent Regency wood stove, its glass front glowing a reassuring orange and red, the popping sounds telling us we would

climbs 1,500 vertical feet over two miles to the structure. It sits at 10,800 feet near the ridge linking Wheeler and Gold Hill (12,711 feet), providing great high-alpine touring in woods or on open slopes.

The **Bull-o-the-Woods Yurt** accommodates ten people comfortably and has a propane cook stove, kitchen utensils, a selection of games, and a wood stove. You bring your own food and drink. Weekends fill early in the season, but weekdays are often available on short notice. It is run by Southwest Nordic Center, which also operates a string of yurts just north of Chama (see above). For details, visit www.southwestnordiccenter.com.

Jemez Mountains

Chicoma Peak (11,561 feet), the highest point in the Jemez range west of Santa Fe, has been skied and spitboarded, but not by many people. It can be a 14-mile round trip, depending on where the snow blocks road access, which requires an overnight stay. But others report approaching by vehicle within two miles of the summit. The access is via Forest Service Road 144 (31 Mile Road) from Española.

Redondo Peak, the Jemez's second-highest point at 11,258 feet, is a challenging, conspicuous siren (easily seen from as far away as Albuquerque), with some large meadows on its eastern face. George Rinker led ski mountaineering ascents of the peak in 1980 and 1981, but it is rarely skied. Access is via the Jemez Caldera National Preserve.

There are numerous other ski-touring and backcountry possibilities in the Jemez. See the Cross-Country Options section for details.

survive this night just east of the Continental Divide.

We ate some snacks, rested, and warmed up. Restored, a companion and I decided to go out and look for some turns, and we pulled on our clothing again. With the inside temperature now at 64 degrees and the outside temperature at two degrees below zero, it felt like we were preparing for a spacewalk or an excursion on Mars, leaving the security of our pod.

We worked our way up, found an opening in the old-growth forest, and dropped gently down into a little clearing, where we each had eight or so fine turns in a foot of light powder before the terrain flattened out. It put a smile on our faces and made all the effort worthwhile. I thought to myself that at a ski area, one would take such turns for granted. But out here, each set was savored, discussed, and filed away in the memory banks.

The next day dawned clear, as a dazzling sun rose over the Sangre de Cristo Range of southern Colorado. We emerged from the yurt to gaze, transfixed, at the sight. To the northeast rose massive Blanca Peak, Colorado's fourth highest, at 14,345 feet. A portion of the huge San Luis Valley lay at our feet, harboring farms, fields, and the town of Alamosa. Close behind us, cliffs towered upward, marking the east-facing base of Jarosa Peak.

After breakfast we headed out, seeking turns. The treeless slopes at the base of the

Jarosa ridge, running more than a mile and holding numerous chutes and bowls, beckoned. Under certain conditions—lots of fresh snow over a frozen base—these slopes could slide, but a recent warm-up and a little new snow meant it was stable, so we climbed upward until it rose too steeply for our comfort levels. Getting hurt out here would require a complex rescue operation, so we played it safe. The snow was excellent, with just a hint of sun crust under three to four inches of wind-deposited fluff, making a very carvable surface. We climbed up, turned, and skied down, making six or eight or even a dozen linked turns, then climbed again and skied down, working our way across the slope, over and over, until our legs were shaking and hunger called us in for a break.

That afternoon, after fueling up and taking a brief nap in our warm nest, we emerged again to sample the deeper powder in the forest below the yurt. The terrain was flatter and the turns harder to find, but each one was like a hieroglyph etched in white that said, "We are grateful and not dead."

Each of Southwest Nordic's yurts has beds for six people (though sticking to four is far more comfortable). Pillows, mattresses, and clean mattress covers are provided, as are all cooking pots, dishes, utensils, and a three-burner propane stove. Water is melted from snow on the stove, so guests need to bring only food, clothing, ski gear, and sleeping bags.

The **Neff Mountain Yurt** is 2.75 miles from the trailhead—the shortest approach distance of Southwest's Cumbres yurts—with a gain of 600 vertical feet. There is some fine skiing off the north and east flanks of nearby Neff Mountain. The **Flat Mountain Yurt** is 4.5 miles in, with a vertical gain of 1,080 feet. It offers 2,500 to 3,000 vertical-foot descents into the Chama River Valley and skiing off the high ridge running between Cumbres Pass and Wolf Creek Pass. The **Trujillo Meadows Yurt** is 4.1 miles in, with a vertical gain of only 380 feet. This yurt is appealing to beginner and novice skiers. The Grouse Creek yurt is also 4.1 miles in, with a vertical gain of 1,000 feet.

The season runs from late November into April. The yurts are typically booked well in advance every weekend. Most are available on short notice on weekdays. Rates run at least $68 to at least $125, depending on days booked at mid- or late season. Additional details on what to bring, trail descriptions, and other information are found on the company website, www.southwestnordiccenter.com, or by phone at 575-758-4761.

Another company, **Cumbres Nordic Adventures**, operates a single yurt, the **Spruce Hole Yurt**, also off NM 17 on Cumbres Pass, 20 miles north of Chama (actually located in Colorado). It is a two-and-a-half-mile ski in to the yurt, with 400 feet vertical gain. Sitting at 10,600 feet, it enjoys a good snowpack and nearby is some excellent open terrain for both beginner and advanced skiers or snowshoers. The yurt itself is exceptionally clean and well maintained, and it has a clear dome in its center with a star-viewing chair set atop a tall pole! Rates run from $95 to $145 a night. No dogs allowed. For details, call 575-756-2746 or visit www.yurtsogood.com.

Other Options Statewide

The **Latir Peaks** north of Red River offers another batch of high peaks for backcountry explorations. Few people venture here, as it is far less known than the Taos area. The access is through the town of Questa and the forest service road to Cabresto Lake.

In the heart of the Pecos Wilderness lies the **Truchas Peaks**, which include a handful of peaks topping 13,000 feet and numerous high-12s. Due to the long approaches required, the peaks are hardly visited even in summer, much less winter. But it has at least one designated run, the aptly named Mail Slot (on the north face of Middle Truchas), which requires roped down-climbing to reach the start.

In a solid winter there are even routes skied on the scary-steep, cliffed west face of the **Sandias**, as well as other destinations in northern New Mexico.

The southern mountains also contain some exciting backcountry possibilities, including **Sierra Blanca Peak** (12,005) just outside Ruidoso, and summits in the remote **Gila**

Wilderness and the **San Mateos**. Many particular routes have never seen a skier. Call it the Wild West.

Resources

Terrific information and photos (if a bit dated) of the state's backcountry outing options can be found at www.summitpost.org/new-mexico-backcountry-skiing/444870.

For guided backcountry adventures, check out Beverly Mountain Guides, led by Marc Beverly, a certified international mountain guide.

For details on current hazards in the snowpack and other backcountry skiing information focused on the Taos area, visit www.taosavalanchecenter.org.

Statewide Travel and Ski Resources

Backcountry Resources and Information:
www.summitpost.org/
new-mexico-backcountry-skiing/444870.

New Mexico Highway Conditions: Visit
www.nmroads.com or call 800-432-4269.

New Mexico State Police: They coordinate all
search-and-rescue operations in the state.
In emergencies, call 911 or a local state
police office.

Santa Fe Search and Rescue: One of the
nation's premier backcountry operations of
its kind. Based in Santa Fe, they operate
statewide, including winter missions. Call
or visit www.santafesar.org.

New Mexico State Tourism Department:
Their free, annual *New Mexico True
Adventure Guide* includes information on
skiing here. Get it at www.newmexico.org.

Ski New Mexico: This nonprofit trade-
industry organization represents New
Mexico's eight downhill ski areas and two
cross-country operations. Its website (www.
skinewmexico.com) provides condition
reports for each area and has other details
about the local ski scene. It also produces a
free annual magazine.

KRQE/CBS-TV: Weatherman Mark
Ronchetti is a hard-core skier and loves
heavy weather. His reporting often includes
storm and skiing videos.

Bibliography

Beard, Sam. *Ski Touring in Northern New
Mexico: A Guide to Ski Touring in the
National Forests of Northern New Mexico and
Certain Areas in Southern Colorado.* 2nd ed.
Albuquerque, NM: Nordic Press, 1988.

Burns, Jim, Cheryl Lemanski, and James
Maki. *Skiing the Sun: Skiing in New Mexico's
National Forests.* Los Alamos, NM: Los
Alamos Ski Touring, 1985.

Holm, Dale, and Bob Skaggs. *50 Years at
Pajarito.* Three-part video produced in 2007
for the Los Alamos Ski Club.

Matthews, Kay. *Cross-Country Skiing in
Northern New Mexico: An Introduction and
Trail Guide.* Chamisal, NM: Acequia Madre
Press, 1986.

Richards, Rick. *Ski Pioneers: Ernie Blake, His
Friends, and the Making of Taos Ski Valley.*
Helena, MT: Dry Gulch Publishing in
association with SkyHouse Publishers
(Falcon Press), 1992.

Salmon, Pamela. *Sandia Peak: A History of
Sandia Peak Tramway and Ski Area.*
Albuquerque, NM: Sandia Peak Ski and
Tramway, 1998.

Photographs

Page 6. One of the prime views at Enchanted Forest reveals the upper Red River Valley and Wheeler Peak on the horizon. Photo courtesy of Enchanted Forest.

Page 8. Jean Mayer displays his solid, energetic, and enthusiastic style on the slopes of Taos Ski Valley. Photo by and courtesy of Peter Lamont.

Page 14. A boarder paints a massive backcountry line in the Waterfall zone near Taos Ski Valley. Photo courtesy Jared Bella.

Page 16. Two snowboarders pause to admire the view of the Moreno Valley below and the distant Sangre de Cristos, including the state's highest summit, Wheeler Peak. Photo courtesy of Angel Fire Resort.

Page 17. A snowboarder sweeps down Exhibition at Angel Fire under the lights in New Mexico's only night skiing operation. Photo courtesy of Angel Fire Resort.

Page 19. All a child at Angel Fire needs to have fun is some snow and sunshine. Photo courtesy of Angel Fire Resort.

Page 20. Kids in the Angel Fire ski school receive some tender, loving encouragement on a snowy day. Photo courtesy of Angel Fire Resort.

Page 21. Skiers on a chair in silhouette at Angel Fire, with the state's highest summit, Wheeler Peak, in the distance. Photo courtesy of Angel Fire Resort.

Page 22. Kids of all ages will enjoy riding the inner tubes at Angel Fire. Photo courtesy of Angel Fire Resort.

Page 23. A skier in golden light cashes in on some of the excellent powder skiing to be found at Angel Fire. Photo courtesy of Angel Fire Resort.

Page 24. A snowboarder performs a trick in Angel Fire's terrain park during its night operation. Photo courtesy of Angel Fire Resort.

Page 26. In the base area rests the Lodge at Angel Fire; above it rise Domingo and Upper Domingo, flanked on the left by a narrow ribbon of Maxwell's Grant. Photo courtesy of Angel Fire Resort.

Page 27. Angel Fire's Liberation Park is perhaps the best in the state. Photo courtesy of Angel Fire Resort.

Page 29. The old "Blue Chair" at Pajarito above a "typical" slope, with the Rio Grande Valley and Sangre de Cristo Range in the background. Photo courtesy of Pajarito Mountain Ski Area.

Page 31. Another crowded powder day at Pajarito riding up one of its older lifts. Photo by the author.

Page 32. Looking off the back side of the ski area into the Valle Grande, heart of the beautiful Jemez Mountains. Photo by the author.

Page 33. The base area beginner slopes at Pajarito are illuminated by a burst of sunshine. Photo courtesy of Pajarito Mountain Ski Area.

Page 33. A contestant gets inverted at one of the annual USASA competitions held at Pajarito. Photo courtesy of Pajarito Mountain Ski Area.

Page 37. Lodging, dining, and Main Street itself is but a stone's throw from the slopes of Red River. Photo courtesy of Megan Gallagher.

Page 39. The small community of Red River is New Mexico's only true "ski town." Photo courtesy of Red River Real Estate. Photo by Rachel Swigart.

Page 41. Collegiate ski racers from around the Rocky Mountains gather annually in Red River for a major race; here they anxiously await posted results. Photo courtesy of Kitty Leaken.

Page 43. In the winter of 2016, Red River hosted its first skijoring event, a wild and wacky race down town streets, with horses pulling racers through the course and over jumps at whip speed. Photo courtesy of Megan Gallagher.

Page 44. The Sandia Peak Tramway 60-passenger cable car emerges near its summit into a wind-blasted snowy realm after the storm has cleared. Photo courtesy of Sandia Peak Tramway Co.

Page 45. A 1950s promotional image taken at Sandia Peak, then called La Madera, plays off the state's Hispanic heritage.

Page 46. Taken from a plane in 1969, this photo captures the summit of Sandia's ski area, with the chairlift in lower center, the top tram station on upper left, and the Summit Haus restaurant and bar. It also reveals the amazing drop off the rim to the desert floor 4,000 feet below. Photo courtesy of Sandia Peak Ski Area.

Page 47. Four women skiers suit up for a race at the then La Madera Ski Area in the 1950s. From left to right: Billie Cotter, Pat Abruzzo, Katy Eckert, and Dona Boyden. Photo courtesy of Sandia Peak Ski Area.

Page 47. Native New Mexican Robert J. Nordhaus, father of La Madera / Sandia Peak and an acclaimed leader of the US ski industry, still ripped it in his elder years, as seen here. Photo courtesy of Sandia Peak Ski Area.

Page 48. Ben Abruzzo, one of the founders of La Madera / Sandia Peak and eventual owner, blasts down Inhibition on a powder day. Photo courtesy of Sandia Peak Ski Area.

Page 48. One of the two Sandia Peak tram

cable cars heads up into the dark and snowy elevations on its run to the top of the ski area. Photo courtesy of Sandia Peak Ski Area.

Page 49. The western-facing snow-crusted rim of the Sandia Mountains curve away to the south and the Manzano range, the alluvial plains sweeping up against their feet. Photo courtesy of Sandia Peak Ski Area.

Page 49. A clear day on Exhibition at Sandia provides awesome views of the westernmost edge of the Great Plains below and the isolated San Pedro and Ortiz Mountains. Photo courtesy of Sandia Peak Ski Area.

Page 54. You've arrived on the right day, to freshies at Sipapu in the Carson National Forest. Photo courtesy of Sipapu Ski and Summer Resort.

Page 55. A look at Upper Gable from the main chair on a bluebird day—not a skier in sight. Photo courtesy of Sipapu Ski and Summer Resort.

Page 56. A typical weekday at Sipapu means empty chairs and slopes, here with a dusting of fresh snow. Photo courtesy of Sipapu Ski and Summer Resort.

Page 56. The New Mexican–born founder and decades-long director of Sipapu, Lloyd Bolander. Photo courtesy of Sipapu Ski and Summer Resort.

Page 57. The powerful New Mexico sun clears the mountain horizon over Sipapu's mellow and nicely groomed beginner slope. Photo courtesy of Sipapu Ski and Summer Resort.

Page 58. A lone boarder sizes up his jump in Sipapu's advanced terrain park, Don Diego. Photo courtesy of Sipapu Ski and Summer Resort.

Page 59. The homey Main Lodge at Sipapu sits on the banks of the Rio Pueblo. Photo courtesy of Sipapu Ski and Summer Resort.

Page 60. The base complex at Ski Apache, including the gondola station in lower left and the iconic original lodge with its soaring spires, faces the wide open intermediate slope Capitan and its quad chair. To the upper center and right run the gondola and Lincoln chair alignments, some of the most sustained pitches on the mountain. Photo courtesy of Ski Apache.

Page 61. A snowboarder under the Apache Arrow gondola on a typically sunny day. Photo courtesy of Ski Apache.

Page 62. A timber rail fence marks the boundary of the ski area under Sierra Blanca (White Mountain) towering above the tree line. Photo by the author.

Page 63. The snow-clad summit of Sierra Blanca Peak rises above the searing sands of the Chihuahua Desert, a remarkable contrast in environments.

Page 64. A bro airs it out above Sierra Blanca Peak. Photo courtesy of Ski Apache.

Page 67. Leg one of the Apache Windrider Ziptour, one of the world's longest zip lines, starts at an elevation of 11,489 feet. Photo courtesy of Ski Apache.

Page 69. A boarder on Gay Way lays down some smooth giant slalom turns far above the snow-covered lowlands to the west. Photo courtesy of Ski Santa Fe.

Page 70. Early January 2016 conditions on Fall Line as seen from the Tesuque Peak chair. Photo by the author.

Page 72. A ski jumper in the 1970s catches some air off the area's many small cliffs, perhaps near bottom of today's Chile Glade. Photo courtesy of Ski Santa Fe.

Page 73. Left to right, Pete Totemoff, Ernie Blake, Robert Nordhaus, and Buzz Bainbridge celebrate old memories at a reunion at Ski Santa Fe. Photo courtesy of Ski Santa Fe.

Page 74 Roadrunner, under the Tesuque Peak triple chair is one of the best mogul runs on the mountain, a real thigh burner with an audience. January 2016. Photo by the author.

Page 75. A boarder snakes out of the woods and into one of Ski Santa Fe's numerous glades. Photo courtesy of Ski Santa Fe.

Page 76. A hard charger pops off and over a heavy mogul field on Dr. Rich. Photo courtesy of Ski Santa Fe.

Page 77. The deck at Totemoff's is a popular, sun-filled space to gather for lunch and adult beverages, with an occasional live band. Photo courtesy of Ski Santa Fe.

Page 77. La Casa Lodge, at the ski area base, was significantly expanded and remodeled in 2015. Photo courtesy of Ski Santa Fe.

Page 81. Kachina Peak at sunset and the runs of one portion of Taos Ski Valley crisscrossing down the mountain, taken from an ultralite. Photo courtesy of Taos Ski Valley. Photo by Chris Dahl Bredine.

Page 82. Garrett Altmann of New Mexico takes it big in the 2012 Taos Freeride Championships, scoring a perfect 10 on this run. Photo courtesy of and by Mo Kaluta.

Page 83. Avalanche dogs, such as Cara and Dana, play an important safety role at TSV and add to the character of the place as well. Photo courtesy of Taos Ski Valley.

Page 85. A snowboarder off West Basin Ridge cranks a turn in the pow. Photo courtesy of Taos Ski Valley.

Page 86. Rhoda Blake raised three kids at TSV, initially in a trailer, while filling many key roles and functions. This is thought to have been taken on her honeymoon in Sun Valley, Idaho. Photo courtesy of Taos Ski Valley.

Page 86. Ernie Blake, TSV founder, hikes above tree line along Highline Ridge, decades before most skiers heard of the words "extreme terrain." Photo courtesy of Taos Ski Valley.

Page 87. A skier airs off a rocky knob on Kachina Peak's primary run, Main Street. To the north stretches the Lake Fork Valley; the base village lies around its bend. Photo courtesy of Taos Ski Valley.

Page 88. Hip-checking some speed in deep powder, the skier eyes the next big, bottomless turn. Photo courtesy of Taos Ski Valley.

Page 89. Cranking giant slalom turns in the forgiving pow of one of the newest sectors of the mountain to open, the fantastic Wild West Glades. Photo courtesy of Taos Ski Valley.

Page 90. Many people are fond of the fondue served up at various Taos locations, including this pot at the Bavarian. Photo courtesy of Taos Ski Valley.

Page 91. Jean Mayer, the founder of the St. Bernard, a great skier and warm soul, oversees the preparation and serving of a meal at the consistently best table in the valley. Photo courtesy of and by Kitty Leaken.

Page 93. The Bavarian, with its convenient location to the Kachina Peak sector, has become an institution among Taos Ski Valley's favored spots to gather for food and beverages on the mountain. Photo courtesy of Taos Ski Valley.

Page 98. Marlise Unger hits her stride at Enchanted Forest through an aspen grove on a bluebird day. Photo courtesy of Enchanted Forest.

Page 100. Two skiers enjoy the nice rolling, groomed trails of the Angel Fire cross-country operation on the grounds of the Angel Fire Country Club. Photo courtesy of Angel Fire Resort.

Page 101. A man and his dog at play at Enchanted Forest, which has a dedicated section devoted to such activity. Photo courtesy of Enchanted Forest.

Page 102. A youngster at Enchanted Forest shows that even kids can enjoy this healthy activity. Photo courtesy of Enchanted Forest.

Page 103. Light, blue shadows and winter grasses form a lovely sight. Photo by the author.

Page 104. Two of the many playful trail names at Enchanted Forest Cross-Country Ski and Snowshoe Area. Photo by the author.

Page 105. One of the prime views at Enchanted Forest reveals the upper Red River Valley and Wheeler Peak on the horizon. Photo courtesy of Enchanted Forest.

Page 107. The author and outstanding guide James Reidy set off on a cross-country jaunt in the high country of the massive Vermejo Park Ranch. Some of the 12,000-foot-plus peaks on the property line the horizon to the west. Photo by Kitty Leaken.

Page 108. Competitors head for the hills at the annual Chama Chile Ski Classic. Photo by and courtesy of Kitty Leaken.

Page 109. The top competitors at the annual Chama Chile Ski Classic, including Clay Moseley (number 50) in retro threads, and Steve Ilg (number 40), line up for the start of a race in January 2016. Photo by the author.

Page 110. The sun sparkles off a small rio in northern New Mexico during a winter warm-up. Photo by the author.

Page 114. Participants in the annual end-of-season pond-skimming contest at TSV include an occasional yeti. Photo courtesy of Taos Ski Valley.

Page 116. A snowboarder passes under the frozen waterfall near the bottom of the long descent off the southeast side of Kachina Peak. Photo courtesy of and by Jared Bella at Taos Imagery.

Page 117. Dogs love the backcountry too, as seen here in the Lake Fork Valley near Taos Ski Valley. Photo courtesy of and by Jared Bella at Taos Imagery.

Page 118. The prime alpine touring enclave of New Mexico, Lake Fork Valley. The east face of Kachina Peak rises in the center, with the runs of Taos Ski Valley to the right. Photo taken from Peace Sign Chute. Photo courtesy of and by Jared Bella at Taos Imagery.

Page 118. It's rough going after surface snow sets up in Wilderness Bowl near Kachina Peak. Photo courtesy of and by Marc Beverly.

Page 119. A panorama of 12,000-foot-plus peaks as seen from the summit of Kachina Peak within Taos Ski Valley's boundary looking to the south. In the center right is Lake Fork Peak. Access to these goods from TSV is forbidden but are skied via a long approach up Lake Fork Valley and a steep climb. Photo by the author.

Page 120. "Spaceship Yurt" glows reassuringly amid the deadly cold near the Continental Divide near Chama. Photo by and courtesy of Kitty Leaken.

Page 120. Skiers approaching the skiing terrain above Grouse Creek yurt north of Chama. Photo by and courtesy of Kitty Leaken.

Page 121. Even the rugged, hard-core, gnarly west face of the Sandias are skied once in a while, as seen in this rare image. Photo courtesy of and by Marc Beverly.

Index

SOUTHWEST ADVENTURE SERIES

Ashley M. Biggers, Series Editor

The Southwest Adventure Series provides practical how-to guidebooks for readers seeking authentic outdoor and cultural excursions that highlight the unique landscapes of the American Southwest. Books in the series feature the best ecotourism adventures, world-class outdoor recreation sites, back-road points of interest, and culturally significant archeological sites, as well as lead readers to the best sustainable accommodations and farm-to-table restaurants in Arizona, Colorado, Nevada, New Mexico, Utah, and Southern California.

Also available in the Southwest Adventure Series:

Eco-Travel New Mexico: 86 Natural Destinations, Green Hotels, and Sustainable Adventures by Ashley M. Biggers